THE LION BOOK OF
CHRISTIAN POETRY

Compiled by Pat Alexander
With biographies by Veronica Zundel

A LION BOOK

Copyright © 1981 Lion Publishing

Published by
Lion Publishing
Icknield Way, Tring, Herts, England
ISBN 0 85648 313 3
Albatross Books
PO Box 320, Sutherland, NSW 2232, Australia
ISBN 0 86760 332 1

First edition 1981
Reprinted 1983
Reprinted 1984

Illustrations
Mark Astle, page 53; Simon Bull, pages 18–19, 24, 93
40, 43, 52, 66, 73, 74, 97, 100, 103, 106; Garet Cousins,
pages 62, 69, 88, 117; Amanda Page, pages 56, 78–9, 82,
83, 110; Stanley Willcocks, pages 55, 105, 119, 121.
Drawings on pages 12, 14, 16, 28, 29, 37, 47, 48, 51, 59, 64,
84, 94 are from *1800 Woodcuts by Thomas Bewick
and his school*, edited by Blanche Cirker, © 1962
Dover Publications Inc.; those on pages 26, 50, 60, 81,
85 are from *A Source Book of French Advertising Art*,
Faber and Faber.
The New England Primer on page 33 is from the New
York Public Library Picture collection.
The illustrations by William Blake (page 44), Gabriel
Dante Rossetti (page 63) and G.H. Lewis (page 70)
are reproduced by permission of The Tate Gallery,
London.
The portrait of Queen Elizabeth I, page 15, engraved
by Crispin Van de Passe, is reproduced by permission
of the National Portrait Gallery, London.
Photographs: on page 10, Lion Publishing/David
Alexander; page 21, Lion Publishing/Jon Willcocks,
by permission of the Dean and chapter of St Paul's
Cathedral, London; page 88, Lion Publishing/Jon
Willcocks.

Cover photo: Malcolm Robertson

Printed in Italy by New Interlitho SPA, Milan

CONTENTS

INTRODUCTION

This book is a 'taster', an appetizer. It is designed as an introduction to the rich heritage of Christian poetry in the English language over a period of 1300 years.

Many, but not all, of the poems included are classics – well known and well loved. The purpose of the book has determined the selection. The choice is concentrated mainly on short poems which will communicate readily to modern readers. Spelling has been modernized, as has the use of capital letters. The selection is very much a personal choice, always enjoyable, sometimes difficult because of the many favourites which have to be left out in a book of this length.

The poems are arranged in order, following the authors' dates of birth. The first poem in the book was composed by the stockman Caedmon in the seventh century and is translated from the original Anglo-Saxon. The book ends with just a small selection from the many excellent modern poets. Christian poetry is very much alive today.

It is the content of the poems themselves, not the Christian standing or theology of the poets, which has determined the selection. Since many of the poets are long-dead, this seems the only practical basis of choice. Poets are in any case by nature individualists, expressing their own unique insights. Sometimes the depth of faith expressed in the poems is surprising in the light of what we know of the poet otherwise.

The disadvantage of selection by content is that it narrows the actual subject-matter, concentrating on the specifically religious dimension of life. But the Christian faith relates to the whole of life. And the hardest decision has been to exclude poems by Christian poets which reflect on nature, human love and the world in general.

This leaves us room for another collection of poems, with fewer poets and a wider-ranging content. This book is simply a starter, one which has given much pleasure in the making, and which it is hoped will bring enjoyment and enrichment of faith to the reader.

CAEDMON

The father of English verse
Late seventh century

Bede, the great Saxon historian of the early English church, tells the story of how Caedmon, a simple cowherd, received God's gift of poetry.

Caedmon could not sing, and when at a feast the harp was passed round for the guests to entertain one another, Caedmon would slip out to the cattle-shed. One night, as he dozed there, he saw in his dreams a man standing beside him.

'Caedmon,' the man said, 'sing me a song.'

'I don't know how to sing,' he replied.

'But you shall sing to me,' came the answer.

'What shall I sing about?' asked the herdsman.

'Sing about the creation of all things.'

And to his own surprise, Caedmon immediately began to sing. When he woke up, he remembered the verses and taught them to his friends. He became a monk at the Abbey of Whitby and there wrote many other poems in praise of God. But only this fragment has survived in writing.

Caedmon's Hymn

Now must we hymn heaven's Guardian,
Might of the Maker and his mind's wisdom,
Work of the glorious Father; how he, eternal Lord,
Made the beginning of every wonder.
He made first, for the sons of men,
Heaven overhead, holy Creator.
Then the mid-earth mankind's Guardian –
Eternal Lord, Almighty God –
Made for man's dwelling.

MEDIEVAL CAROLS

The earliest carols were songs to accompany a round dance, and for this reason Christians tended to frown on them. By the fourteenth century carols had become respectable, and were used in church processions, particularly at the very popular feast of Christmas. Bible story, legend and everyday details were freely mixed in these songs, which often gave the delightful impression that the birth of Christ was a local news item! Many of the Christmas carols we still sing today date back as far as the fifteenth century. The earliest surviving collection of them was printed by Wynkyn de Worde in 1521.

I Saw Three Ships

I saw three ships come sailing in,
  On Christmas Day, on Christmas Day,
I saw three ships come sailing in,
  On Christmas Day in the morning.
And what was in those ships all three?
Our Saviour Christ and his lady.
Pray, whither sailed those ships all three?
O, they sailed into Bethlehem.
And all the bells on earth shall ring,
And all the angels in heaven shall sing,
And all the souls on earth shall sing.
Then let us all rejoice amain!

Some carols were specially written for the 'miracle' plays performed at church festivals by the town guilds, the medieval trade unions. The plays presented Bible stories in a contemporary setting, with a great deal of humour. At Coventry, which in the fifteenth century was a centre of England's wool trade, the pageant of the Shearmen and Tailors included this carol, sung by the women of Bethlehem before Herod's massacre of the children.

The Coventry Carol

Lully, lulla, thou little tiny child,
By by, lully lullay.
O sisters too,
How may we do
   For to preserve this day
This poor youngling,
For whom we do sing,
   By by, lully lullay?

Herod, the king,
In his raging,
   Charged he hath this day
His men of might,
In his own sight,
   All young children to slay.

That woe is me,
Poor child for thee!
   And ever morn and day,
For thy parting
Neither say nor sing
   By by, lully lullay!

This carol was discovered in an old church-gallery book in Dorset, England.

Rejoice and Be Merry

Rejoice and be merry in songs and in mirth!
O praise our Redeemer, all mortals on earth!
For this is the birthday of Jesus our King,
Who brought us salvation – his praises we'll sing!

A heavenly vision appeared in the sky;
Vast numbers of angels the shepherds did spy,
Proclaiming the birthday of Jesus our King,
Who brought us salvation – his praises we'll sing!

Likewise a bright star in the sky did appear,
Which led the Wise Men from the east to draw near;
They found the Messiah, sweet Jesus our King,
Who brought us salvation – his praises we'll sing!

And when they were come, they their treasures unfold,
And unto him offered myrrh, incense, and gold.
So blessèd for ever be Jesus our King,
Who brought us salvation – his praises we'll sing.

EDMUND SPENSER

1552?–1599

During the reign of Queen Elizabeth I a group of talented young men formed themselves into a literary circle, with Spenser as their leading light. His masterpiece, written in Ireland where he had been presented with a castle, was 'The Faerie Queene'. This long poem, left half-finished, with only six books of the planned twelve written, uses the knights of medieval romance to celebrate the chivalric ideals of Elizabethan England. At its heart stands Queen Gloriana, a tribute to Elizabeth herself. Spenser married another Elizabeth, who is addressed in this sonnet for Easter Day.

'Most Glorious Lord of Life'

Most glorious Lord of life, that on this day
   Didst make thy triumph over death and sin;
   And having harrowed hell didst bring away
   Captivity thence captive, us to win:
This joyous day, dear Lord, with joy begin,
   And grant that we for whom thou diddest die
   Being with thy dear blood clean washed from sin,
   May live for ever in felicity.
And that thy love we weighing worthily,
   May likewise love thee for the same again;
   And for thy sake that all like dear didst buy,
   With love may one another entertain.
So let us love, dear love, like as we ought.
Love is the lesson which the Lord us taught.

SIR WALTER RALEIGH
1552?–1618

Raleigh, the famous explorer and adventurer, was knighted after discovering Virginia, which he named after Elizabeth I, the Virgin Queen. In 1592 he fell from favour by secretly marrying the queen's lady-in-waiting. He was imprisoned in the Tower of London and sentenced to death. He was reprieved, but after the queen's death he was in prison again, for an alleged plot against the new king, James I. Once again Raleigh was freed, and allowed to go on a final expedition. When this failed, he was arrested and executed. This poem was probably written during one of his imprisonments.

The Pilgrimage

Give me my scallop shell of quiet,
My staff of faith to walk upon,
My scrip of joy, immortal diet,
My bottle of salvation:
My gown of glory, hope's true gauge,
And thus I'll take my pilgrimage.

Blood must be my body's balmer,
No other balm will there be given,
Whilst my soul like a white palmer
Travels to the land of heaven,
Over the silver mountains,
Where spring the nectar fountains:
And there I'll kiss
The bowl of bliss,
And drink my eternal fill
On every milken hill.
My soul will be a-dry before,
But after it, will ne'er thirst more.

And by the happy blissful way
More peaceful pilgrims I shall see,
That have shook off their gowns of clay,
And go apparelled fresh like me.
I'll bring them first
To slake their thirst,
And then to taste those nectar suckets
At the clear wells
Where sweetness dwells,
Drawn up by saints in crystal buckets.

And when our bottles and all we,
Are filled with immortality:
Then the holy paths we'll travel
Strewed with rubies thick as gravel,
Ceilings of diamonds, sapphire floors,
High walls of coral and pearl bowers.

From thence to heaven's bribeless hall
Where no corrupted voices brawl,
No conscience molten into gold,
Nor forged accusers bought and sold,
No cause deferred, nor vain spent journey,
For there Christ is the king's attorney:
Who pleads for all without degrees,
And he hath angels, but no fees.

When the grand twelve million jury,
Of our sins with sinful fury,
Gainst our souls black verdicts give,
Christ pleads his death, and then we live,
Be thou my speaker, taintless pleader,
Unblotted lawyer, true proceeder,
Thou movest salvation even for alms:
Not with a bribed lawyer's palms.

And this is my eternal plea,
To him that made heaven, earth and sea,
Seeing my flesh must die so soon,
And want a head to dine next noon.
Just at the stroke when my veins start and spread
Set on my soul an everlasting head.
Then am I ready like a palmer fit,
To tread those blest paths which before I writ.

ROBERT SOUTHWELL

1561–1595

Southwell came from a Roman Catholic family at a time when Catholics were regarded as traitors to the English crown. After his education in Paris and Rome, he returned to England as a priest with the English Mission, a secret campaign to restore the country to Catholicism. He managed to evade capture for six years, but in 1592 he was arrested on his way to celebrate Mass for his patroness the Countess of Arundel. He was imprisoned in the Tower of London for three years, tortured thirteen times and finally hanged on the infamous Tyburn gallows. But the poems published immediately after his death lived on.

A Child My Choice

Let folly praise that fancy love, I praise and love that Child
Whose heart no thought, whose tongue no word, whose hand no deed defiled.
I praise him most, I love him best, all praise and love is his;
While him I love, in him I live, and cannot live amiss.
Love's sweetest mark, laud's highest theme, man's most desired light,
To love him life, to leave him death, to live in him delight.
He mine by gift, I his by debt, thus each to other due,
First friend he was, best friend he is, all times will try him true.

The Nativity of Christ

Behold the father is his daughter's son,
The bird that built the nest is hatched therein,
The old of years an hour hath not outrun,
Eternal life to live doth now begin,
The Word is dumb, the mirth of heaven doth weep,
Might feeble is, and force doth faintly creep.

O dying souls, behold your living spring;
O dazzled eyes, behold your sun of grace;
Dull ears, attend what word this Word doth bring;
Up, heavy hearts, with joy your joy embrace.
From death, from dark, from deafness, from despairs,
This life, this light, this Word, this joy repairs.

Gift better than himself God doth not know;
Gift better than his God no man can see.
This gift doth here the giver given bestow;
Gift to this gift let each receiver be.
God is my gift, himself he freely gave me;
God's gift am I, and none but God shall have me.

Man altered was by sin from man to beast;
Beast's food is hay, hay is all mortal flesh.
Now God is flesh and lies in manger pressed
As hay, the brutest sinner to refresh.
O happy field wherein this fodder grew,
Whose taste doth us from beasts to men renew.

JOHN DONNE
1571(?2)–1631

Donne is the greatest of the 'metaphysical' poets of the seventeenth century, whose poetry is marked by striking images, wit and intellectual complexity. His promising career as secretary to Sir Thomas Egerton, 'keeper of the great seal', was cut short by a secret marriage to Egerton's niece, Anne More. After sailing on two expeditions Donne became an Anglican priest. He was later appointed Dean of St Paul's Cathedral, London. There he preached a series of great sermons, many of them before King Charles I. His statue, for which he posed in his shroud, can be seen in St Paul's today. If we may believe his many 'profane' poems, Donne had a succession of mistresses in his youth. A deep sense of repentance marks his later religious poems, such as the first below, where he puns on his own name (pronounced 'Dunne').

A Hymn to God the Father

Wilt thou forgive that sin where I begun,
  Which is my sin, though it were done before?
Wilt thou forgive those sins through which I run,
  And do them still, though still I do deplore?
    When thou hast done, thou has not done,
      For I have more.

Wilt thou forgive that sin by which I won
  Others to sin, and made my sin their door?
Wilt thou forgive that sin which I did shun
  A year or two, but wallowed in a score?
    When thou hast done, thou has not done,
      For I have more.

I have a sin of fear, that when I've spun
  My last thread, I shall perish on the shore;
Swear by thyself that at my death thy Sun
  Shall shine as it shines now, and heretofore;
    And having done that, thou hast done,
      I have no more.

On Death

Death, be not proud, though some have called thee
Mighty and dreadful, for thou art not so;
For those whom thou thinkst thou dost overthrow
Die not, poor Death, nor yet canst thou kill me.
From rest and sleep, which but thy pictures be,
Much pleasure – then, from thee much more must flow;
And soonest our best men with thee do go,
Rest of their bones and soul's delivery.
Thou'rt slave to fate, chance, kings, and desperate men,
And dost with poison, war, and sickness dwell;
And poppy or charms can make us sleep as well,
And better than thy stroke. Why swellst thou then?
One short sleep past, we wake eternally,
And death shall be no more. Death, thou shalt die.

'Teach Me How to Repent'

At the round earth's imagined corners blow
Your trumpets, angels, and arise, arise
From death, you numberless infinities
Of souls, and to your scattered bodies go:
All whom the flood did, and fire shall o'erthrow,
All whom war, dearth, age, agues, tyrannies,
Despair, law, chance hath slain, and you whose eyes
Shall behold God and never taste death's woe.
But let them sleep, Lord, and me mourn a space,
For if above all these my sins abound,
'Tis late to ask abundance of thy grace
When we are there. Here on this lowly ground
Teach me how to repent; for that's as good
As if thou hadst sealed my pardon with thy blood.

BEN JONSON

1572–1637

As a young man Jonson was apprenticed to his step-father, a master bricklayer. But he ran away, first to fight the Spaniards in Holland and then to become a rather second-rate actor. He was much more successful as a playwright, particularly with his satirical plays performed at the Court of King James I. William Shakespeare acted in Jonson's first successful play and was one of his friends. Jonson was a fiery character. He once killed a fellow actor in a duel, and narrowly escaped execution. After all his books and manuscripts were tragically destroyed in a fire, he suffered a stroke and lost his place as the Court's most popular entertainer. Nevertheless he was buried in Westminster Abbey, with the epitaph, 'O Rare Ben Jonson'.

A Hymn to God the Father

Hear me, O God!
  A broken heart
  Is my best part:
Use still thy rod
  That I may prove
  Therein thy love.

If thou hadst not
  Been stern to me,
  But left me free,
I had forgot
  Myself and thee.

For sin's so sweet,
  As minds ill bent
  Rarely repent,
Until they meet
  Their punishment.

Who more can crave
  Than thou hast done,
  That gav'st a son
To free a slave,
  First made of nought,
  With all since bought?

Sin, Death, and Hell
  His glorious Name
  Quite overcame,
Yet I rebel,
  And slight the same.

But I'll come in,
  Before my loss
  Me farther toss,
As sure to win
  Under his cross.

WILLIAM AUSTIN

1587–1634

Austin, a lawyer, published few writings. Most of these were religious prose works, such as his 'Certayne Devout, Godly and Learned Meditations'. One was an essay on 'the excellency of the creation of woman' – an unusual choice of subject in view of the prevailing religious attitudes of his time.

There is a modern choral setting of the first of these two Christmas poems, which vividly evokes the shrill but joyous sound of the crowing cock that heralds the nativity.

Chanticleer

All this night shrill chanticleer,
Day's proclaiming trumpeter,
Claps his wings and loudly cries,
Mortals, mortals, wake and rise!
   See a wonder
   Heaven is under;
From the earth is risen a Sun
Shines all night, though day be done.

Wake, O earth, wake everything!
Wake and hear the joy I bring;
Wake and joy; for all this night
Heaven and every twinkling light,
   All amazing,
   Still stand gazing.
Angels, Powers, and all that be,
Wake, and joy this Sun to see.

Hail, O Sun, O blessed Light,
Sent into the world by night!
Let thy rays and heavenly powers
Shine in these dark souls of ours;
   For most duly
   Thou art truly
God and man, we do confess:
Hail, O Sun of Righteousness!

GILES FLETCHER

1588?–1623

Giles Fletcher the younger came from an eminent literary family. His cousin John collaborated with Francis Beaumont to produce some outstanding plays. Giles moved from a post as Reader in Greek Literature at Cambridge University, to become rector of the small town of Alderton in Suffolk. By his own confession, however, he was never happy among the 'country clodhoppers'. His poetry imitates the allegorical style of Spenser, in which each character represents a particular quality, and he was a considerable influence on Milton.

On the Crucifixion

It was but now their sounding clamours sung,
Blessed is he, that comes from the most high,
And all the mountains with Hosanna rung,
And now, away with him, away they cry,
And nothing can be heard but crucify:
   It was but now, the crown itself they save,
   And golden name of king unto him gave,
And now, no king, but only Caesar, they will have:

It was but now they gathered blooming May,
And of his arms disrobed the branching tree,
To strew with boughs, and blossoms all thy way,
And now, the branchless trunk a cross for thee,
And May, dismayed, thy coronet must be:
   It was but now they were so kind, to throw
   Their own best garments, where thy feet should go,
And now, thyself they strip, and bleeding wounds they show.

See where the author of all life is dying:
O fearful day! he dead, what hope of living?
See where the hopes of all our lives are buying:
O cheerful day! they bought, what fear of grieving?
Love love for hate, and death for life is giving:
   Lo how his arms are stretched abroad to grace thee,
   And, as they open stand, call to embrace thee,
Why stay'st thou then my soul; o fly, fly, thither haste thee.

ROBERT HERRICK

1591–1674

For ten years Herrick was apprenticed to follow his father into the goldsmith's craft. He gave this up to go to Cambridge University and prepare for the ministry. For many years he was Vicar of Dean Prior in Devon. He was thrown out by Cromwell because he was a Royalist. When the monarchy returned in 1662 he was reinstated. Described as 'the most frankly pagan of the English poets', he is best known for his love poems and light-hearted works. He wrote the famous 'Gather Ye Rosebuds While Ye May'. Herrick insisted, however, that his life was not to be judged by his verse.

No Coming to God Without Christ

Good and great God! How should I fear
To come to thee, if Christ not there!
Could I but think, he would not be
Present, to plead my cause for me;
To hell I'd rather run, than I
Would see thy face, and he not by.

Grace For Children

What God gives, and what we take,
'Tis a gift for Christ his sake:
Be the meal of beans and peas,
God be thanked for those, and these.
Have we flesh, or have we fish,
All are fragments from his dish.
He his church save, and the king,
And our peace here, like a spring,
Make it ever flourishing.

Another Grace For a Child

Here a little child I stand,
Heaving up my either hand;
Cold as paddocks though they be,
Here I lift them up to thee,
For a benison to fall
On our meat, and on us all.

GEORGE HERBERT
1593–1633

A classical scholar and musician, Herbert started his career as Public Orator at Cambridge University. This was followed by a short time at Court. But when two of his patrons died Herbert decided to be ordained. For the rest of his life he was a conscientious and well-loved parish priest at Bemerton in Wiltshire. 'The Temple', his collection of religious poems, quickly sold 20,000 copies – a large number at that time. Several of them have become popular hymns; they show a warm, genuine faith and an unassuming character. In his prose work, 'A Priest to the Temple', Herbert paints his picture of the ideal local clergyman; it could almost be a self-portrait.

Love

Love bade me welcome; yet my soul drew back,
    Guilty of dust and sin.
But quick-eyed Love, observing me grow slack
    From my first entrance in,
Drew nearer to me, sweetly questioning,
    If I lacked anything.

'A guest', I answered, 'worthy to be here.'
    Love said, 'You shall be he.'
'I, the unkind, ungrateful? Ah, my dear,
    I cannot look on thee.'
Love took my hand, and smiling did reply,
    'Who made the eyes but I?'

'Truth, Lord, but I have marred them; let my shame
    Go where it doth deserve.'
'And know you not', says Love, 'who bore the blame?'
    'My dear, then I will serve.'
'You must sit down', says Love, 'and taste my meat.'
    So I did sit and eat.

The Pulley

When God at first made man,
Having a glass of blessings standing by,
'Let us,' said he, 'pour on him all we can;
Let the world's riches, which dispersèd lie,
    Contract into a span.'

So strength first made a way;
Then beauty flowed, then wisdom, honour, pleasure;
When almost all was out, God made a stay,
Perceiving that, alone of all his treasure,
    Rest in the bottom lay.

'For if I should,' said he,
'Bestow this jewel also on my creature,
He would adore my gifts instead of me,
And rest in nature, not the God of nature:
    So both should losers be.

'Yet let him keep the rest,
But keep them with repining restlessness;
Let him be rich and weary, that at least,
If goodness lead him not, yet weariness
    May toss him to my breast.'

Redemption

Having been tenant long to a rich Lord,
    Not thriving, I resolved to be bold,
    And make a suit unto him, to afford
A new small-rented lease, and cancel the old.
In heaven at his manor I him sought:
    They told me there that he was lately gone
    About some land, which he had dearly bought
Long since on earth, to take possession.
I straight returned, and knowing his great birth,
    Sought him accordingly in great resorts:
    In cities, theatres, gardens, parks, and courts.
At length I heard a ragged noise and mirth
    Of thieves and murderers: there I him espied,
    Who straight, *Your suit is granted*, said, and died.

The Twenty-third Psalm

The God of love my Shepherd is,
And he that doth me feed,
While he is mine, and I am his,
What can I want or need?

He leads me to the tender grass,
Where I both feed and rest;
Then to the streams that gently pass:
In both I have the best.

Or if I stray, he doth convert,
And bring my mind in frame:
And all this not for my desert.
But for his holy name.

Yea, in death's shady black abode
Well may I walk, not fear;
For thou art with me, and thy rod
To guide, thy staff to bear.

Nay, thou dost make me sit and dine
Even in my enemies' sight;
My head with oil, my cup with wine
Runs over day and night.

Surely thy sweet and wondrous love
Shall measure all my days;
And as it never shall remove,
So neither shall my praise.

Jesu

Jesu is in my heart, his sacred name
Is deeply carved there: but the other week
A great affliction broke the little frame
Even all to pieces; which I went to seek:
And first I found the corner where was *J*,
After where *ES*, and next where *U* was graved.
When I had got these parcels, instantly
I sat me down to spell them, and perceived
That to my broken heart he was *I ease you*,
      And to my whole is *JESU*.

This anonymous poem with its highly unusual opening is a favourite reading for Christmas services. It gives a vivid picture of a well-run wealthy household in Jacobean England. A 'dazie' was a type of canopy supported by posts.

The Guest

Yet if his Majesty, our sovereign lord,
Should of his own accord
Friendly himself invite,
And say, 'I'll be your guest tomorrow night',
How should we stir ourselves, call and command
All hands to work! 'Let no man idle stand!

'Set me fine Spanish tables in the hall;
See they be fitted all;
Let there be room to eat
And order taken that there want no meat.
See every sconce and candlestick made bright,
That without tapers they may give a light.

'Look to the presence: are the carpets spread,
The dazie o'r the head,
The cushions in the chairs,
And all the candles lighted on the stairs?
Perfume the chambers, and in any case
Let each man give attendance in his place!'

Thus, if a king were coming, would we do;
And 'twere good reason too;
For 'tis a duteous thing
To show all honour to an earthly king,
And after all our travail and our cost,
So he be pleased, to think no labour lost.

But at the coming of the King of heaven
All's set at six and seven;
We wallow in our sin,
Christ cannot find a chamber in the inn.
We entertain him always like a stranger,
And, as at first, still lodge him in the manger.

JOHN MILTON
1608–1674

After Chaucer and Shakespeare, Milton is surely the best-known and greatest English poet. Unlike many others, he saw poetry as his 'vocation'.

Milton had already written several of his best poems when he became involved in politics, and began to write pamphlets on a wide range of subjects: church government, education, the freedom of the press, divorce. (His young wife had left him to go home at the start of the Civil War — though she later returned. According to Dr Johnson, she 'seems not to have delighted in the pleasures of spare diet and hard study'.)

During Cromwell's rule, Milton was Latin Secretary to the government. At the restoration of the monarchy he was arrested, but let off with a heavy fine. By this time he was completely blind. Yet it was at this stage, having written very little poetry for twenty years, that he produced his masterpiece, 'Paradise Lost'. But 'the call for books was not in Milton's age what it is at present,' writes Johnson. After two years, with a sale of only 1300 copies, Milton had received a total payment of £10.

On His Blindness

When I consider how my light is spent,
Ere half my days, in this dark world and wide,
And that one talent which is death to hide
Lodged with me useless, though my soul more bent
To serve therewith my Maker, and present
My true account, lest he returning chide,
'Doth God exact day-labour, light denied?'
I fondly ask. But Patience, to prevent
That murmur, soon replies: 'God doth not need
Either man's work or his own gifts; who best
Bear his mild yoke, they serve him best. His state
Is kingly: thousands at his bidding speed,
And post o'er land and ocean without rest;
They also serve who only stand and wait.'

ANNE BRADSTREET
1612–1672

Anne Bradstreet was the first significant poet in American literature. She was born in England and had a Puritan upbringing. At sixteen she married, and two years later left England aboard the 'Arbella' with her husband and parents. Her father became leader and later governor of the colony in Massachusetts. The Bradstreets settled on a farm near the frontier village of Andover. Anne did not take easily to such a primitive existence. She had first to be 'convinced it was the way of God'. Somehow, despite all the household chores and bringing up a family of eight children, she managed to keep a little time for reading and writing poetry, even though the community did not approve of women poets.

In 1647 her brother-in-law took copies of her poems with him to England – and they were published there without Anne's knowledge; the first book of poems by a settler in the colonies. No American woman poet could match Anne's lyrics, until Emily Dickinson, 200 years later.

As Spring the Winter

As spring the winter doth succeed
And leaves the naked trees do dress,
The earth all black is clothed in green.
At sunshine each their joy express.

My sun's returned with healing wings,
My soul and body doth rejoice,
My heart exults and praises sings
To him that heard my wailing voice.

My winter's past, my storms are gone,
And former clouds seem now all fled,
But if they must eclipse again,
I'll run where I was succoréd.

I have a shelter from the storm,
A shadow from the fainting heat,
I have access unto his throne,
Who is a God so wondrous great.

O hath thou made my pilgrimage
Thus pleasant, fair, and good,
Blessed me in youth and elder age,
My Baca made a springing flood.

O studious am what I shall do
To show my duty with delight;
All I can give is but thine own
And at the most a simple mite.

A

In *Adam's* Fall
We Sinned all.

B

Thy Life to Mend
This *Book* Attend.

C

The *Cat* doth play
And after flay.

D

A *Dog* will bite
A Thief at night.

An *Eagles* flight
Is out of fight.

The Idle *Fool*
Is whipe at School.

RICHARD BAXTER

1615–1691

Baxter has been called 'the creator of popular Christian literature' for his book 'The Saints' Everlasting Rest'. It is mentioned in George Eliot's novel 'The Mill on the Floss' as one character's favourite reading in a domestic crisis!

Baxter lived through one of the stormiest periods of English history. He acted as adviser to Cromwell and served as chaplain to the Parliamentary soldiers in the Civil War. He represents Puritanism at its best. Although he was a minister of the Church of England, because he would not declare that ordination by a bishop was essential, or that the Book of Common Prayer was perfect beyond improvement (a requirement of the 1662 'Act of Uniformity'), he became a 'nonconformist', persecuted, imprisoned and forbidden to preach.

In 1685, aged seventy and suffering from tuberculosis, he was sentenced to eighteen months in prison by the tyrannical Judge Jeffreys. This poem witnesses to his courage in an unstable world.

Lord, it Belongs Not to My Care

Lord, it belongs not to my care,
  Whether I die or live;
To love and serve thee is my share,
  And this thy grace must give.

If life be long I will be glad,
  That I may long obey;
If short – yet why should I be sad
  To soar to endless day?

Christ leads me through no darker rooms
  Than he went through before;
He that unto God's kingdom comes,
  Must enter by this door.

Come, Lord, when grace has made me meet
  Thy blessed face to see;
For if thy work on earth be sweet,
  What will thy glory be!

Then I shall end my sad complaints,
  And weary, sinful days;
And join with the triumphant saints,
  To sing Jehovah's praise.

My knowledge of that life is small,
  The eye of faith is dim;
But 'tis enough that Christ knows all,
  And I shall be with him.

HENRY VAUGHAN

1622–1695

Henry Vaughan was nicknamed 'the Silurist' because of his love for his native county of Brecknockshire in Wales (once inhabited by the Silures). He studied law at Oxford and in London – then changed from law to medicine and returned to Wales as a doctor. Vaughan may have served as a surgeon in the English Civil War. He was certainly an ardent supporter of the king, and fought on the king's side. He and his twin brother Thomas were imprisoned for their Royalist sympathies. Vaughan's spiritual life was suddenly deepened after a serious illness, and from then on he wrote only religious poetry and tried to suppress his earlier, more light-hearted works.

Easter Hymn

Death and darkness get you packing,
Nothing now to man is lacking,
All your triumphs now are ended,
And what Adam marred is mended;
Graves are beds now for the weary,
Death a nap, to wake more merry;
Youth now, full of pious duty,
Seeks in thee for perfect beauty,
The weak, and aged tired, with length
Of days, from thee look for new strength,
And infants with thy pangs contest
As pleasant, as if with the breast;
Then, unto him, who thus hath thrown
Even to contempt thy kingdom down,
And by his blood did us advance
Unto his own inheritance,
To him be glory, power, praise,
From this, unto the last of days.

JOHN BUNYAN

1628–1688

John Bunyan is known the world over as the author of 'The Pilgrim's Progress', the story of Christian's journey from the City of Destruction to the Celestial City. Born in a Bedfordshire village, Bunyan had little education and followed his father into the tinsmith's trade. At sixteen, during the Civil War, he was drafted into the Parliamentary Army. When he returned home he married a woman as poor as himself. Her only dowry was two books: 'The Plain Man's Pathway to Heaven' and 'The Practice of Piety'. These awoke a longing in Bunyan's heart which led, after much inner struggle, to his conversion. He became a travelling Baptist preacher. At that time all noncomformist meetings were illegal. Bunyan was arrested, held in Bedford prison for six years, released briefly, then held for six years more – until a change in the law made it possible for him to have a preacher's licence. It was while he was in prison that he started to write.

The Shepherd Boy's Song

He that is down, needs fear no fall;
   He that is low, no pride;
He that is humble ever shall
   Have God to be his guide.

I am content with what I have,
   Little be it or much;
And, Lord, contentment still I crave,
   Because thou savest such.

Fulness to such a burden is,
   That go on pilgrimage;
Here little, and hereafter bliss,
   Is best from age to age.

The Pilgrim's Song

Who would true valour see,
    Let him come hither;
One here will constant be,
    Come wind, come weather;
There's no discouragement
Shall make him once relent
His first avowed intent
        To be a pilgrim.

Whoso beset him round
    With dismal stories,
Do but themselves confound;
    His strength the more is.
No lion can him fright,
He'll with a giant fight,
But he will have a right
        To be a pilgrim.

Hobgoblin nor foul fiend
    Can daunt his spirit;
He knows he at the end
    Shall life inherit.
Then fancies fly away,
He'll not fear what men say;
He'll labour night and day
        To be a pilgrim.

EDWARD TAYLOR

1642?–1729

In his early twenties Edward Taylor left England and emigrated to Massachusetts. He studied at Harvard University (founded just a few decades earlier) in preparation for the ministry. A strict Puritan, he became pastor and doctor at the farming village of Westfield, 100 miles west of Boston. He spent the remaining fifty-eight years of his life in this frontier post.

At his own request his poems were not published during his lifetime and his grandson, Ezra Stiles, put them in Yale University for safe-keeping. They remained there for 200 years — until they were 'discovered' in 1937. They were published two years later. Taylor wrote in the tradition of the 'metaphysical' poets. They were, in his own words, 'ragged rhymes', produced by a 'tattered fancy'. Others have judged them among the best of early American writing.

Huswifery

Make me, O Lord, thy spinning wheel complete.
   Thy holy word my distaff make for me.
Make mine affections thy swift flyers neat,
   And make my soul thy holy spool to be.
   My conversation make to be thy reel,
   And reel the yarn thereon spun off thy wheel.
Make me thy loom then, knit therein this twine;
   And make thy holy spirit, Lord, wind quills;
Then weave the web thyself. The yarn is fine.
   Thine ordinances make my fulling mills.
   Then dye the same in heavenly colors choice,
   All pinked with varnished flowers of paradise.

Then clothe therewith mine understanding, will,
   Affections, judgement, conscience, memory,
My words and actions, that their shine may fill
   My ways with glory and thee glorify.
   Then mine apparel shall display before ye
   That I am clothed in holy robes for glory.

ISAAC WATTS

1674–1748

Isaac Watts' schoolmaster father had been in prison for his nonconformist views. Although exceptionally gifted (he had begun learning Latin at the age of four) Isaac too threw in his lot with the 'Dissenters'. He refused an offer from a local doctor to pay his university fees because places were limited to members of the established church. Instead he became the pastor of Mark Lane Chapel, London. 'Such was he as every Christian Church would rejoice to have adopted,' wrote Dr Johnson. 'In the pulpit, though his low stature, which very little exceeded five feet, graced him with no advantages of appearance, yet the gravity and propriety of his utterance made his discourses very efficacious.'

When he first began to write hymns they had to be called out to the congregation line by line. When they were published they were immensely popular and ran into sixteen editions in his lifetime alone. He still ranks as one of the greatest and most popular of English hymn-writers. Several lines from his 'Divine Songs for Children', the first children's hymnbook, have passed into common usage as proverbs.

'From All That Dwell Below the Skies'

From all that dwell below the skies
Let the Creator's praise arise;
Let the Redeemer's name be sung
Through every land by every tongue.

Eternal are thy mercies, Lord;
Eternal truth attends thy word:
Thy praise shall sound from shore to shore,
Till suns shall rise and set no more.

In every land begin the song;
To every land the strains belong:
In cheerful sounds all voices raise
And fill the world with loudest praise.

From 'A Cradle Song'

Hush! my dear, lie still and slumber,
   Holy angels guard thy bed!
Heavenly blessings without number
   Gently falling on thy head.

Sleep, my babe; thy food and raiment,
   House and home, thy friends provide;
All without thy care or payment,
   All thy wants are well supplied.

How much better thou'rt attended
   Than the Son of God could be,
When from heaven he descended,
   And became a child like thee!

Soft and easy is thy cradle:
   Coarse and hard thy Saviour lay:
When his birthplace was a stable,
   And his softest bed was hay.

JOHN BYROM

1692–1763

After a short time as a medical student, John Byrom began to teach his own system of shorthand, invented while he was at Cambridge University. His class in Manchester was attended by, among others, the writer Horace Walpole and the politician Lord Chesterfield. Pupils, who paid five guineas for their lessons, had to swear that they would keep the method secret. It was not published until after Byrom's death. Byrom wrote both religious and humorous poetry, and contributed essays to Addison's magazine 'The Spectator'. His well-known hymn 'Christians Awake' was written as a present for his daughter.

'My Spirit Longeth For Thee'

My spirit longeth for thee
   Within my troubled breast;
Although I be unworthy
   Of so divine a Guest.

Of so divine a Guest,
   Unworthy though I be;
Yet has my heart no rest,
   Unless it come from thee.

Unless it come from thee,
   In vain I look around;
In all that I can see,
   No rest is to be found.

No rest is to be found,
   But in thy blessed love;
O, let my wish be crowned,
   And send it from above.

WILLIAM COWPER

1731–1800

William Cowper suffered all his life from an over-sensitive, depressive nature. He studied law, but the stress of attempting a public career led to serious depression, attempted suicide and his first attack of madness.

It was after he recovered that Cowper became a Christian. He moved to Olney in Buckinghamshire, where John Newton was curate, and contributed a number of poems to the 'Olney Hymns'. The simple and gentle faith expressed in his hymns shines all the brighter against their dark background.

Sadly the friendship with Newton aggravated Cowper's illness. Newton, with more good intent than understanding, forced the extremely shy Cowper to help in his evangelistic work. Only after Newton left Olney did Cowper achieve a measure of stability, helped by gardening, carpentry, and his tame hares and pet spaniel.

It was his friend Lady Austen who suggested he should write about these simple things around him. The result is some of the finest English poetry about nature.

'Oh! For a Closer Walk With God'

Oh! for a closer walk with God,
  A calm and heavenly frame;
A light to shine upon the road
  That leads me to the Lamb!

Where is the blessedness I knew
  When first I saw the Lord?
Where is the soul-refreshing view
  Of Jesus and his word?

What peaceful hours I once enjoyed!
  How sweet their memory still!
But they have left an aching void,
  The world can never fill.

Return, O holy Dove, return,
  Sweet messenger of rest;
I hate the sins that made thee mourn,
  And drove thee from my breast.

The dearest idol I have known,
  Whate'er that idol be;
Help me to tear it from thy throne,
  And worship only thee.

So shall my walk be close with God,
  Calm and serene my frame;
So purer light shall mark the road
  That leads me to the Lamb.

WILLIAM BLAKE

1757–1827

William Blake was apprenticed to an engraver at fourteen and later studied art at the Royal Academy in London. A natural rebel, he was soon dissatisfied with the Academy's narrow approach.

It was in the year of the storming of the Bastille that Blake produced his 'Songs of Innocence', a collection of poems which express the spirit of childhood. He printed these by hand, with his own illustrations, and his wife Catherine bound them. The 'Songs of Experience', some of which were designed as contrasts to the earlier book, followed.

Blake had a passion for liberty. This love of freedom and dislike of conventional morality made him one of the idols of the modern hippie movement.

He was an artist, a mystic and visionary. Beneath the apparent simplicity of his poems is a great intensity of feeling.

The Lamb

Little Lamb, who made thee?
Dost thou know who made thee?
Gave thee life, and bid thee feed
By the stream and o'er the mead;
Gave thee clothing of delight,
Softest clothing, woolly, bright;
Gave thee such a tender voice,
Making all the vales rejoice?
Little Lamb, who made thee?
Dost thou know who made thee?

Little Lamb, I'll tell thee,
Little Lamb, I'll tell thee:
He is called by thy name,
For he calls himself a Lamb.
He is meek, and he is mild;
He became a little child.
I a child, and thou a lamb,
We are called by his name.
Little Lamb, God bless thee!
Little Lamb, God bless thee!

On Another's Sorrow

Can I see another's woe,
And not be in sorrow too?
Can I see another's grief,
And not seek for kind relief?

Can I see a falling tear,
And not feel my sorrow's share?
Can a father see his child
Weep, nor be with sorrow filled?

Can a mother sit and hear
An infant groan, an infant fear?
No, no! never can it be!
Never, never can it be!

And can he who smiles on all
Hear the wren with sorrows small,
Hear the small bird's grief and care,
Hear the woes that infants bear,

And not sit beside the nest,
Pouring pity in their breast;
And not sit the cradle near,
Weeping tear on infant's tear;

And not sit both night and day,
Wiping all our tears away?
O, no! never can it be!
Never, never can it be!

He doth give his joy to all;
He becomes an infant small;
He becomes a man of woe;
He doth feel the sorrow too.

Think not thou canst sigh a sigh
And thy maker is not by;
Think not thou canst weep a tear
And thy maker is not near,

O! he gives to us his joy
That our grief he may destroy;
Till our grief is fled and gone
He doth sit by us and moan.

The Clod and the Pebble

'Love seeketh not itself to please,
'Nor for itself hath any care,
'But for another gives its ease,
'And builds a heaven in hell's despair.'

So sung a little clod of clay
Trodden with the cattle's feet,
But a pebble of the brook
Warbled out these metres meet:

'Love seeketh only self to please,
'To bind another to its delight,
'Joys in another's loss of ease,
'And builds a hell in heaven's despite.'

The Divine Image

To Mercy, Pity, Peace, and Love
All pray in their distress;
And to these virtues of delight
Return their thankfulness.

For Mercy, Pity, Peace, and Love
Is God, our father dear,
And Mercy, Pity, Peace, and Love
Is man, his child and care.

For Mercy has a human heart,
Pity a human face,
And Love, the human form divine,
And Peace, the human dress.

Then every man, of every clime,
That prays in his distress,
Prays to the human form divine,
Love, Mercy, Pity, Peace.

And all must love the human form,
In heathen, Turk, or Jew,
Where Mercy, Love and Pity dwell
There God is dwelling too.

JOHN CLARE

1793–1864

John Clare went to school only three months each year. The other nine he spent herding geese and sheep on his father's Northampton-shire farm. Later he took work as a farm labourer, going to night school in his spare time. While he worked in the fields he would note down ideas on the crown of his hat and later work them into verses which are paintings in words of the countryside and its creatures. At last he saved enough money to publish a collection, and was an instant sensation as 'the peasant poet'. Lord Radstock became his patron and gave him a regular income to set up his own farm. By this time, however, Clare was married and soon had a large family. He was not a good organizer and, sadly, money worries finally drove him to an asylum.

I Am

I am – yet what I am none cares or knows,
   My friends forsake me like a memory lost;
I am the self-consumer of my woes,
   They rise and vanish in oblivions host,
Like shadows in love – frenzied stifled throes
And yet I am, and live like vapours tossed

Into the nothingness of scorn and noise,
   Into the living sea of waking dreams,
Where there is neither sense of life or joys,
   But the vast shipwreck of my life's esteems;
And e'en the dearest – that I love the best –
Are strange – nay, rather stranger than the rest.

I long for scenes where man has never trod,
   A place where woman never smiled or wept;
There to abide with my Creator, God,
   And sleep as I in childhood sweetly slept:
Untroubling and untroubled where I lie,
The grass below – above the vaulted sky.

Nature's Hymn to the Deity

All nature owns with one accord
The great and universal Lord:
The sun proclaims him through the day,
The moon when daylight drops away,
The very darkness smiles to wear
The stars that show us God is there,
On moonlight seas soft gleams the sky,
And, 'God is with us,' waves reply.

Winds breathe from God's abode, 'We come,'
Storms louder own God is their home,
And thunder yet with louder call,
Sounds, 'God is mightiest over all';
Till earth, right loath the proof to miss,
Echoes triumphantly, 'He is,'
And air and ocean makes reply,
'God reigns on earth, in air and sky.'

All nature owns with one accord
The great and universal Lord:
Insect and bird and tree and flower –
The witnesses of every hour –
Are pregnant with his prophecy
And, 'God is with us,' all reply.
The first link in the mighty plan
Is still – and all upbraideth man.

WILLIAM CULLEN BRYANT

1794–1878

This precocious young man was reading conservative New England newspapers at five. By the age of eight he was already writing devotional poems. His first poem was published in 1807 – he had written and recited it at school when he was nine. He came from a long line of New England ministers. He studied and practised law, while his poems won increasing recognition. In 1825 he left Massachusetts, and the law, for New York. There he joined the editorial staff of the 'New York Evening Post', of which he became part-owner and editor-in-chief for fifty years.

He campaigned for the end of slavery, free speech, the rights of labour. He backed political reform, and helped found the Republican party – supporting Lincoln and the Union cause during the Civil War.

His best poems, written in the 1840s, evoke the prairie landscape and New England countryside – soft and gentle nature.

To a Waterfowl

Whither, midst falling dew,
While glow the heavens with the last steps of day,
Far, through their rosy depths, dost thou pursue
    Thy solitary way?

Vainly the fowler's eye
Might mark thy distant flight to do thee wrong,
As, darkly seen against the crimson sky,
    Thy figure floats along.

Seek'st thou the plashy brink
Of weedy lake, or marge of river wide,
Or where the rocking billows rise and sink
    On the chafed ocean-side?

There is a Power whose care
Teaches thy way along that pathless coast –
The desert and illimitable air –
    Lone wandering, but not lost.

All day thy wings have fanned,
At that far height, the cold, thin atmosphere,
Yet stoop not, weary, to the welcome land,
    Though the dark night is near.

And soon that toil shall end;
Soon shalt thou find a summer home, and rest,
And scream among thy fellows; reeds shall bend,
    Soon, o'er thy sheltered nest.

Thou'rt gone, the abyss of heaven
Hath swallowed up thy form; yet, on my heart
Deeply has sunk the lesson thou hast given,
    And shall not soon depart.

He who, from zone to zone,
Guides through the boundless sky thy certain flight,
In the long way that I must tread alone,
    Will lead my steps aright.

—ELIZABETH BARRETT BROWNING—
1806–1861

The fairy-tale romance of Elizabeth Barrett and Robert Browning is well known through the play 'The Barretts of Wimpole Street'. But Elizabeth was already a popular English poet long before she met Browning. Indeed she was a child prodigy, reading Homer in the original Greek at eight and publishing an epic poem at fourteen. A combination of parental strictness, spinal injury and grief at her favourite brother's death made her an invalid, though she continued to write in her darkened room. It was her poetry that brought Browning to visit her; and in 1846 they eloped, an action which made Elizabeth's jealous father disown her. The couple were however blissfully happy. They lived in Florence, where Elizabeth's health recovered greatly and where she wrote her famous love poems, 'Sonnets from the Portuguese'.

Patience Taught By Nature

'O dreary life,' we cry, 'O dreary life!'
And still the generations of the birds
Sing through our sighing and the flocks and herds
Serenely live while we are keeping strife
With heaven's true purpose in us, as a knife
Against which we may struggle! ocean girds
Unslackened the dry land, savannah-swards
Unweary sweep – hills watch, unworn; and rife
Meek leaves drop yearly from the forest-trees,
To show above the unwasted stars that pass
In their old glory. O thou God of old,
Grant me some smaller grace than comes to these! –
But so much patience as a blade of grass
Grows by, contented through the heat and cold.

50

RICHARD CHEVENIX TRENCH

1807–1886

Writing was a family tradition for Richard Trench. His brother was an essayist and his Irish mother, Melesina, published remarkable journals of her travels in Europe. Trench first wrote poetry to take his mind off his own ill-health and depression while studying at Cambridge University. He became Dean of Westminster Abbey in London and later Archbishop of Dublin. But he still found time to add to his poems a wide range of other writings, including books on the parables and miracles of Jesus; 'Sacred Latin Poetry', a study of ancient hymns; and 'The Study of Words', a pioneer work on linguistics. His lifelong interest in language led him to suggest the scheme for the enormous 'Oxford English Dictionary'.

God Our Refuge

If there had anywhere appeared in space
   Another place of refuge where to flee,
Our hearts had taken refuge in that place,
    And not with thee.

For we against creation's bars had beat
   Like prisoned eagles, through great worlds had sought
Though but a foot of ground to plant our feet,
    Where thou wert not.

And only when we found in earth and air,
   In heaven or hell, that such might nowhere be –
That we could not flee from thee anywhere,
    We fled to thee.

–HENRY WADSWORTH LONGFELLOW–

1807–1882

As a child in Portland, Maine, Longfellow showed more interest in reading than in playing games. This early academic promise continued. He was appointed Professor of Modern Languages immediately after graduating from Bowdoin University, and went on to take up a similar post at Harvard. His poetry was immensely popular in his lifetime; but although he is best known for poems such as 'Hiawatha', 'Paul Revere's Ride', 'The Village Blacksmith' and 'The Wreck of the Hesperus', he considered his lesser-known religious trilogy 'Christus' to be his greatest achievement.

Christmas Bells

I heard the bells on Christmas day
Their old familiar carols play,
 And wild and sweet
 The words repeat,
Of 'Peace on earth, good will to men!'

And thought how, as the day had come,
The belfries of all Christendom
 Had rolled along
 The unbroken song,
Of 'Peace on earth, good will to men!'

Till ringing, singing on its way,
The world revolved from night to day –
 A voice, a chime,
 A chant sublime,
Of 'Peace on earth, good will to men!'

And in despair I bowed my head;
'There is no peace on earth,' I said,
 'For hate is strong
 And mocks the song
Of peace on earth, good will to men!'

Then pealed the bells more loud and deep:
'God is not dead; nor doth he sleep!
 The wrong shall fail,
 The right prevail,
With peace on earth, good will to men!'

ROBERT BROWNING

1812–1889

Robert Browning decided on his career at seventeen. He asked his father, a bank clerk in London, whether the family income was enough to support him in 'a life of pure culture'. On hearing that it was, he became a poet. After the failure of his first published work, a long love poem, he developed his characteristic style, the dramatic monologue. In this he uses one speaker – often in a medieval setting – to explore philosophical or historical ideas. Browning went on to write volume upon volume, enjoying huge successes with such poems as 'Home Thoughts from Abroad' and 'The Pied Piper of Hamelin'. A Browning Society was even formed during his lifetime. Browning was an unorthodox but convinced Christian and only the death of his beloved wife Elizabeth was enough to shake his immense optimism.

Pippa's Song

The year's at the spring,
And day's at the morn;
Morning's at seven;
The hill-side's dew-pearled;
The lark's on the wing;
The snail's on the thorn:
God's in his heaven –
All's right with the world!

JONES VERY

1813–1880

Apart from a brief spell as a classics tutor at Harvard University, Jones Very never left his birthplace of Salem, Massachusetts, where he lived a quiet and retired life with his two sisters. In spite of his acute shyness, he became a Unitarian minister and preached hundreds of sermons. His poems, which were published only occasionally in a few Christian magazines, bear a strong resemblance to the work of seventeenth-century 'metaphysical' poets such as Donne and Herbert. Very was a friend of the famous American writer and visionary Ralph Waldo Emerson, who rescued him from a stay in an asylum by declaring that Very was 'profoundly sane'.

The Prayer

Wilt thou not visit me?
The plant beside me feels thy gentle dew,
   And every blade of grass I see
From thy deep earth is quickening moisture drew.

   Wilt thou not visit me?
Thy morning calls on me with cheering tone;
   And every hill and tree
Lend but one voice – the voice of Thee alone.

   Come, for I need thy love,
More than the flower the dew or grass the rain;
   Come, gently as thy holy dove;
And let me in thy sight rejoice to live again.

   I will not hide from them
When thy storms come, though fierce may be their wrath,
   But bow with leafy stem,
And strengthened follow on thy chosen path.

   Yes, thou wilt visit me:
Nor plant nor tree thine eye delights so well,
   As, when from sin set free,
My spirit loves with thine in peace to dwell.

HENRY DAVID THOREAU

1817–1862

*'The man I meet is seldom as instructive as the silence he breaks.'
This wry remark typifies Thoreau's individualist attitude to life.
Harvard classics scholar, Orientalist, student of Red Indian culture, and naturalist, Thoreau left his academic career to discover a
more simple and self-sufficient lifestyle. Earning a meagre living by
casual outdoor labour, he built himself a log cabin in the woods of
Massachusetts. His autobiographical book 'Walden, or life in the
woods' became a textbook of the 'back to nature' movement.*

Inspiration

Whate'er we leave to God, God does,
And blesses us;
The work we choose should be our own,
God lets alone.

EMILY BRONTE
1818–1848

Few authors can have achieved such fame as Emily Bronte with such a small output: one novel and a handful of poems. Yet millions have been stirred by the grandeur of her tragic love story, 'Wuthering Heights'. With her sisters Charlotte and Anne, brother Branwell and widowed father, Emily lived in an isolated parsonage on the Yorkshire moors in the north of England. The sisters' only entertainment was writing, and they each produced masterpieces. Emily's main inspiration was the wild moorland landscape she loved passionately. The stormiest of the Brontes, Emily hated rules and restraint. Already suffering from tuberculosis, she caught a cold at her brother's funeral, but refused to see a doctor or even to rest. She died only months later, defiant to the last.

Last Lines

No coward soul is mine,
No trembler in the world's storm-troubled sphere:
I see Heaven's glories shine,
And faith shines equal, arming me from fear.

O God within my breast,
Almighty, ever-present Deity!
Life – that in me has rest,
As I – undying Life – have power in thee!

Vain are the thousand creeds
That move men's hearts: unutterably vain;
Worthless as withered weeds,
Or idle froth amid the boundless main,

To waken doubt in one
Holding so fast by thine infinity;
So surely anchored on
The steadfast rocks of immortality.

With wide-embracing love
Thy spirit animates eternal years,
Pervades and broods above,
Changes, sustains, dissolves, creates, and rears.

Though earth and man were gone,
And suns and universes ceased to be,
And thou were left alone,
Every existence would exist in thee.

There is not room for death,
Nor atom that his might could render void:
Thou – thou art being and breath,
And what thou art may never be destroyed.

JOHN MASON NEALE

1818–1866

One eighth of all the hymns in the Church of England hymnbook, 'Hymns Ancient and Modern', come from the pen of John Mason Neale. Some are original works, and some translations of early church hymns. Neale's career in the church suffered because of his links with the Oxford Movement, a campaign to reinstate traditional pre-Reformation practices and doctrines. Neale became warden of Sackville College, a refuge for old men, where his redecoration of the chapel was condemned by the bishop as 'spiritual haberdashery'. His many writings range from stories and sermons for children to such oddities as 'A History of Pews' and 'Hymns for Use During the Cattle Plague'.

'Light's Glittering Morn'

Light's glittering morn bedecks the sky;
Heaven thunders forth its victor-cry;
The glad earth shouts her triumph high,
And groaning hell makes wild reply;

While he, the King, the mighty King,
Despoiling death of all its sting,
And, trampling down the powers of night,
Brings forth his ransom'd saints to light.

His tomb of late the threefold guard
Of watch and stone and seal had barred;
But now, in pomp and triumph high,
He comes from death to victory.

The pains of hell are loosed at last;
The days of mourning now are past;
An angel robed in light hath said,
'The Lord is risen from the dead.'

EMILY DICKINSON

1830–1886

Slowly but steadily, since the publication of 'Poems by Emily Dickinson' in 1890 (four years after her death), Emily Dickinson has won a place among the greatest of all American lyric poets.

Her immediate world was narrow. She spent all her life at Amherst where she was born, with little stimulus at home ('Mother does not care for thought') and no firsthand contact with important contemporary writers. Her neighbours saw this strange moth-like apparition, dressed all in white, simply as an eccentric maiden lady.

But emotion and imagination know no bounds. Emily's passionate sensitivity was expressed in almost 1800 poems, found neatly tied in packets after her death. Love, death, nature, beauty are all explored, in metres familiar from Protestant hymn books. She early rebelled against her Calvinist background, struggling for a balance between faith and scepticism. As she grew older she became even more withdrawn, writing, and looking on at life from her bedroom window.

I Never Saw a Moor

I never saw a moor,
I never saw the sea;
Yet know I how the heather looks,
And what a wave must be.

I never spoke with God,
Nor visited in Heaven;
Yet certain am I of the spot
As if the chart were given.

Because I Could Not Stop For Death

Because I could not stop for Death,
He kindly stopped for me;
The carriage held but just ourselves
And Immortality.

We slowly drove, he knew no haste,
And I had put away
My labor, and my leisure too,
For his civility.

We passed the school where children played,
Their lesson scarcely done;
We passed the fields of gazing grain,
We passed the setting sun.

We paused before a house that seemed
A swelling on the ground;
The roof was scarcely visible,
The cornice but a mound.

Since then 'tis centuries; but each
Feels shorter than the day
I first surmised the horses' heads
Were toward eternity.

CHRISTINA ROSSETTI

1830–1894

Daughter of a distinguished Italian political refugee, and younger sister of painter and poet Dante Gabriel Rossetti, Christina Rossetti lived in London all her life. Her first collection of poems was printed by her grandfather when she was twelve. Later she published in magazines under the name of Ellen Alleyne. Her fantasy poems for children as well as her religious poems won wide acclaim. Christina's faith was deep and central to her life. She was talented and pretty, but twice refused offers of marriage from men she loved, because she could not agree with them on matters of religion. At a less serious level, she even pasted strips of paper over passages in Swinburne's poetry which she considered 'irreligious'. Her life was spent caring for her widowed mother and in serving the needy.

'If Only'

If I might only love my God and die!
But now he bids me love him and live on,
Now when the bloom of all my life is gone,
The pleasant half of life has quite gone by.
My tree of hope is lopped that spread so high;
And I forget how summer glowed and shone,
While autumn grips me with its fingers wan,
And frets me with its fitful windy sigh.
When autumn passes then must winter numb,
And winter may not pass a weary while,
But when it passes spring shall flower again:
And in that spring who weepeth now shall smile,
Yea, they shall wax who now are on the wane,
Yea, they shall sing for love when Christ shall come.

'If I Could Trust Mine Own Self'

If I could trust mine own self with your fate,
    Shall I not rather trust it in God's hand?
    Without whose will one lily doth not stand,
Nor sparrow fall at his appointed date;
    Who numbereth the innumerable sand,
Who weighs the wind and water with a weight,
To whom the world is neither small nor great,
    Whose knowledge foreknew every plan we planned.
Searching my heart for all that touches you,
    I find there only love and love's goodwill
Helpless to help and impotent to do,
Of understanding dull, of sight most dim;
And therefore I commend you back to him
    Whose love your love's capacity can fill.

A Better Resurrection

I have no wit, no words, no tears;
    My heart within me like a stone
Is numbed too much for hopes or fears.
    Look right, look left, I dwell alone;
I lift mine eyes, but dimmed with grief
    No everlasting hills I see;
My life is in the falling leaf:
    O Jesus, quicken me.

My life is like a faded leaf,
    My harvest dwindled to a husk:
Truly my life is void and brief
    And tedious in the barren dusk;
My life is like a frozen thing,
    No bud nor greenness can I see;
Yet rise it shall – the sap of Spring;
    O Jesus, rise in me.

My life is like a broken bowl,
    A broken bowl that cannot hold
One drop of water for my soul
    Or cordial in the searching cold;
Cast in the fire the perished thing;
    Melt and remould it, till it be
A royal cup for him, my King:
    O Jesus, drink of me.

'O Lord, Seek Us'

O Lord, seek us, O Lord, find us
   In thy patient care;
Be thy love before, behind us,
   Round us, everywhere:
Lest the god of this world blind us,
   Lest he speak us fair,
Lest he forge a chain to bind us,
   Lest he bait a snare.
Turn not from us, call to mind us,
   Find, embrace us, bear;
Be thy love before, behind us,
   Round us, everywhere.

THOMAS EDWARD BROWN

1830–1897

The son of a poor clergyman in the Isle of Man, Brown went to Oxford University, but as a 'servitor' – a student who received financial aid for waiting on wealthier students, and was treated as a second-class citizen. Perhaps it was this humbling experience that helped him, when he became a schoolmaster and curate in Bristol, to relate to all classes of people. Fellow-poet W.E. Henley described him as 'cynic, saint, salt, humorist, Christian, poet ... with a heart large as St Francis'. Brown wrote many of his poems in the Manx dialect of his home.

My Garden

A garden is a lovesome thing, God wot!
Rose plot,
Fringed pool,
Ferned grot –
The veriest school
Of peace; and yet the fool
Contends that God is not –
Not God! in gardens! when the eve is cool?
Nay, but I have a sign;
'Tis very sure God walks in mine.

NEGRO SPIRITUALS

American settlers started to import Africans as slaves in the seventeenth century, and their numbers increased enormously until slavery was outlawed in 1808. The slaves were taught Christianity by white missionaries and evangelists. It is not surprising that they identified strongly with the children of Israel in captivity. They expressed their emotions in song, adapting Methodist hymns, and the choruses sung at religious camp-meetings, to their own African rhythms. The result was a gutsy, honest style which paved the way for the later ragtime, blues and jazz as well as gospel songs. Spirituals were popularized by travelling choirs such as the Fisk University Jubilee Singers formed in 1871. Since that time they have often been rendered bland, robbed of their distinctiveness and emotional content. But they remain universally popular.

Go Tell

When I was a learner,
   I sought both night and day.
I ask the Lord to help me,
   An' he show me the way, the way.
Go tell it on de mountains;
Ober de hills an' ev'ry where:
Go tell it on de mountains,
Our Jesus Christ is born.

And he made me a watchman;
   Up on the city wall,
An' if I am a Christian;
   I am the least of all, of all.
Go tell it on de mountains,
Ober de hills an' ev'ry where,
Go tell it on de mountains,
Our Jesus Christ is born.
Our Jesus Christ is born.

Go Down, Moses

When Israel was in Egypt's land:
Let my people go,
Oppressed so hard they could not stand,
Let my people go.
Go down, Moses,
Way down in Egypt's land,
Tell ole Pharaoh,
Let my people go.

Thus saith the Lord, bold Moses said,
Let my people go.
If not, I'll smite your first-born dead,
Let my people go.

No more shall they in bondage toil,
Let my people go,
If them come out with Egypt's spoil,
Let my people go.

O let us all from bondage flee,
Let my people go,
And let us all in Christ be free,
Let my people go.

66

1842–1881

Lanier, who was born in Macon, Georgia, volunteered for service in the American Civil War and fought with the confederates for four years. He was taken prisoner and contracted the tuberculosis which was to kill him. The war, however, also produced his first writing: 'Tiger Lilies', a war novel. While lecturing in English literature at Johns Hopkins University, he achieved popularity with 'Corn', a long poem on Southern agriculture. He was also a gifted musician, first flautist with the Peabody Symphony Orchestra, Baltimore. And his poem 'The Symphony' imitates the effects of the various instruments – violin, clarinet, flute, horn, bassoon – in verse.

A Ballad of Trees and the Master

Into the woods my Master went,
Clean forspent, forspent.
Into the woods my Master came,
Forspent with love and shame.
But the olives they were not blind to him,
The little gray leaves were kind to him:
The thorn-tree had a mind to him
   When into the woods he came.

Out of the woods my Master went,
And he was well content.
Out of the woods my Master came,
Content with death and shame.
When death and shame would woo him last,
From under the trees they drew him last:
'Twas on a tree they slew him – last
   When out of the woods he came.

GERARD MANLEY HOPKINS
1844–1889

'What fun if you were a classic!' Hopkins remarked to his lifelong friend, the poet Robert Bridges, at a time when his own poems were not even published. Coming from a high church background, Hopkins was received into the Roman Catholic church by Dr Newman at Oxford. He joined the Jesuits – and burnt all the verses he had written.

After nine years training he worked as a priest and teacher in several British towns. But the poverty and squalor of the industrial towns, and his own poor health, depressed him.

In 1875, after much inward debate, he began again to write poetry, using the new rhythm and creative, innovative use of language which gives his verse such power. He made no attempt to publish anything. Not until 1918, long after his death, did Robert Bridges edit and publish his work. Hopkins was in fact so far ahead of his time that the delay in publication probably gave the poems a much better chance of success.

God's Grandeur

The world is charged with the grandeur of God.
  It will flame out, like shining from shook foil;
  It gathers to a greatness, like the ooze of oil
Crushed. Why do men then now not reck his rod?
Generations have trod, have trod, have trod;
  And all is seared with trade; bleared, smeared with toil;
  And wears man's smudge and shares man's smell: the soil
Is bare now, nor can foot feel, being shod.

And for all this, nature is never spent;
  There lives the dearest freshness deep down things;
And though the last lights off the black West went
  Oh, morning, at the brown brink eastward, springs –
Because the Holy Ghost over the bent
  World broods with warm breast and with ah! bright wings.

Pied Beauty

Glory be to God for dappled things –
    For skies of couple-colour as a brinded cow;
      For rose-moles all in stipple upon trout that swim;
Fresh firecoal chestnut-falls; finches' wings;
    Landscapes plotted and pieced — fold, fallow, and plough;
    And all trades, their gear and tackle and trim.

All things counter, original, spare, strange;
    Whatever is fickle, freckled (who knows how?)
      With swift, slow; sweet, sour; adazzle, dim;
He fathers-forth whose beauty is past change:
                  Praise him.

Spring

Nothing is so beautiful as spring –
    When weeds, in wheels, shoot long and lovely and lush;
    Thrush's eggs look little low heavens, and thrush
Through the echoing timber does so rinse and wring
The ear, it strikes like lightnings to hear him sing;
    The glassy peartree leaves and blooms, they brush
    The descending blue; that blue is all in a rush
With richness; the racing lambs too have fair their fling.

What is all this juice and all this joy?
    A strain of the earth's sweet being in the beginning
In Eden garden. – Have, get, before it cloy,
    Before it cloud, Christ, lord, and sour with sinning,
Innocent mind and Mayday in girl and boy,
    Most, O maid's child, thy choice and worthy the winning.

Hurrahing in Harvest

Summer ends now; now, barbarous in beauty, the stooks arise
    Around; up above, what wind-walks! what lovely behaviour
    Of silk-sack clouds! has wilder, wilful-wavier
Meal-drift moulded ever and melted across skies?

I walk, I lift up, I lift up heart, eyes,
    Down all that glory in the heavens to glean our Saviour;
    And, eyes, heart, what looks, what lips yet gave you a
Rapturous love's greeting of realer, of rounder replies?

And the azurous hung hills are his world-wielding shoulder
    Majestic – as a stallion stalwart, very-violet-sweet! –
These things, these things were here and but the beholder
    Wanting; which two when they once meet,
The heart rears wings bold and bolder
    And hurls for him, O half hurls earth for him off under his feet.

The Windhover

To Christ our Lord

I caught this morning morning's minion,
    kingdom of daylight's dauphin, dapple-dawn-drawn Falcon,
      in his riding
    Of the rolling level underneath him steady air, and
      striding
High there, how he rung upon the rein of a wimpling wing
In his ecstasy! then off, off forth on swing,
    As a skate's heel sweeps smooth on a bow-bend! the hurl
      and gliding
    Rebuffed the big wind. My heart in hiding
Stirred for a bird, – the achieve of, the mastery of the thing!

Brute beauty, and valour and act, oh, air, pride, plume, here
    Buckle! AND the fire that breaks from thee then, a billion
Times told lovelier, more dangerous, O my chevalier!

    No wonder of it: sheer plod makes plough down sillion
Shine, and blue-bleak embers, ah my dear,
    Fall, gall themselves, and gash gold-vermilion.

Peace

When will you ever, Peace, wild wooddove, shy wings shut,
Your round me roaming end, and under be my boughs?
When, when, Peace, will you, Peace? I'll not play hypocrite
To own my heart: I yield you do come sometimes; but
That piecemeal peace is poor peace. What pure peace allows
Alarms of wars, the daunting wars, the death of it?

O surely, reaving Peace, my Lord should leave in lieu
Some good! And so he does leave Patience exquisite,
That plumes to Peace thereafter. And when Peace here does house
He comes with work to do, he does not come to coo,
       He comes to brood and sit.

'No Worst, There is None'

No worst, there is none. Pitched past pitch of grief,
More pangs will, schooled at forepangs, wilder wring.
Comforter, where, where is your comforting?
Mary, mother of us, where is your relief?
My cries heave, herds-long; huddle in a main, a chief
Woe, world-sorrow; on an age-old anvil wince and sing –
Then lull, then leave off. Fury had shrieked 'No ling-
ering! Let me be fell: force I must be brief'.

   O the mind, mind has mountains; cliffs of fall
Frightful, sheer, no-man-fathomed. Hold them cheap
May who ne'er hung there. Nor does long our small
Durance deal with that steep or deep. Here! creep
Wretch, under a comfort serves in a whirlwind: all
Life death does end and each day dies with sleep.

ALICE MEYNELL
1847–1922

Although she was born in England, Alice Meynell spent much of her childhood in Italy. She spoke fluent Italian and French. She published her first volume of verse when she was twenty-eight. In 1877 she met and married the writer Wilfred Meynell, and from then on helped him to edit two magazines. The Meynells were poor but hospitable; their uncarpeted, frugal house was a meeting-place for many famous writers of the day (and home to the poet Francis Thompson whom they rescued from starvation). Alice was an ardent feminist and called herself a Christian Socialist. She was once put forward for the Poet Laureateship, the highest honour Britain can accord to a poet.

'I Am the Way'

    Thou art the Way.
Hadst thou been nothing but the goal,
      I cannot say
If thou hadst ever met my soul.

    I cannot see –
I, child of process – if there lies
      An end for me,
Full of repose, full of replies.

    I'll not reproach
The road that winds, my feet that err.
      Access, approach
Art thou, Time, Way, and Wayfarer.

Unto Us a Son is Given

Given, not lent,
And not withdrawn – once sent,
This Infant of mankind, this One,
Is still the little welcome Son.

New every year,
New born and newly dear,
He comes with tidings and a song,
The ages long, the ages long;

Even as the cold
Keen winter grows not old,
As childhood is so fresh, foreseen,
And spring in the familiar green.

Sudden as sweet
Come the expected feet.
All joy is young, and new all art,
And he, too, whom we have by heart.

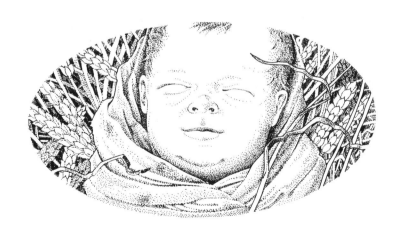

DIGBY MACKWORTH DOLBEN

1848–1867

Dolben went to the famous English public school of Eton, where the future Poet Laureate, Robert Bridges, was his supervisor. On leaving school Dolben became a Benedictine monk, though he was never formally received into the Roman Catholic church because of his father's disapproval. Three years later, while he was preparing for his Oxford entrance exams, he went swimming in the River Welland in Lincolnshire, with a small boy on his back, and was drowned. Robert Bridges edited his devotional poems, all written at school, in 1915.

'I Asked For Peace'

I asked for Peace –
  My sins arose,
  And bound me close,
I could not find release.

I asked for Truth –
  My doubts came in,
  And with their din
They wearied all my youth.

I asked for Love –
  My lovers failed,
  And griefs assailed
Around, beneath, above.

I asked for thee –
  And thou didst come
  To take me home
Within thy heart to be.

ROBERT LOUIS STEVENSON

1850–1894

Born in Edinburgh, Scotland, Stevenson was the son and grandson of lighthouse builders. He too was destined to be an engineer but because of a lung weakness he studied law instead. He started writing after travelling in Europe (where he also met Fanny Osbourne, a married American ten years his senior, who later divorced to marry him). While living in California after his marriage he wrote his first bestseller, 'Treasure Island'. This was followed by several other successful novels both for adults and children, and a book of children's poetry, 'A Child's Garden of Verses'. After travelling all over the world in search of a healthier climate, Stevenson settled in Samoa where he lived for the rest of his life.

The Celestial Surgeon

If I have faltered more or less
In my great task of happiness;
If I have moved among my race
And shown no glorious morning face;
If beams from happy human eyes
Have moved me not; if morning skies,
Books, and my food, and summer rain
Knocked on my sullen heart in vain:
Lord, thy most pointed pleasure take
And stab my spirit broad awake;
Or, Lord, if too obdurate I,
Choose thou, before that spirit die,
A piercing pain, a killing sin,
And to my dead heart run them in!

FRANCIS THOMPSON

1859–1907

Francis Thompson was born in Lancashire, England. He was brought up as a Roman Catholic and intended for the priesthood, but his headmaster thought he was too unstable. So his father, a doctor, sent him to Manchester to study medicine. After six years, having failed his finals three times, he gave up. He ran away to London, became addicted to opium, survived by selling newspapers and matches and slept rough each night near Covent Garden market, where down-and-outs still gather today. He had just decided against killing himself with an overdose when he spotted one of his poems published in a magazine edited by fellow-Catholic Wilfred Meynell. Meynell and his wife Alice rescued Thompson and restored him to health in a Sussex monastery, where he wrote his best works before his early death of tuberculosis.

In No Strange Land

The Kingdom of God is Within You

O world invisible, we view thee,
O world intangible, we touch thee,
O world unknowable, we know thee,
Inapprehensible, we clutch thee!

Does the fish soar to find the ocean,
The eagle plunge to find the air –
That we ask of the stars in motion
If they have rumour of thee there?

Not where the wheeling systems darken,
And our benumbed conceiving soars! –
The drift of pinions, would we hearken,
Beats at our own clay-shuttered doors.

The angels keep their ancient places; –
Turn but a stone, and start a wing!
'Tis ye, 'tis your estranged faces,
That miss the many-splendoured thing.

But (when so sad thou canst not sadder)
Cry; – and upon thy so sore loss
Shall shine the traffic of Jacob's ladder
Pitched betwixt Heaven and Charing Cross.

Yea, in the night, my Soul, my daughter,
Cry, – clinging Heaven by the hems;
And lo, Christ walking on the water,
Not of Gennesareth, but Thames!

To a Snowflake

What heart could have thought you? –
Past our devisal
(O filigree petal!)
Fashioned so purely,
Fragilely, surely,
From what Paradisal
Imagineless metal,
Too costly for cost?
Who hammered you, wrought you,
From argentine vapour? –

'God was my Shaper.
Passing surmisal,
He hammered, he wrought me,
From curled silver vapour,
To lust of his mind: –
Thou couldst not have thought me!
So purely, so palely,
Tinily, surely,
Mightily, fraily,
Insculped and embossed,
With his hammer of wind,
And his graver of frost'.

MARY COLERIDGE

1861–1907

Not only was Mary Coleridge the great-niece of the great English poet Samuel Taylor Coleridge, but she had another poet, W. J. Cory, as her tutor. With literary connections like these it is not surprising that she began to write as a small child. By the time she was twenty, she was already contributing to magazines. Her first collection of poetry, however, was not published until she was thirty-five, and during her lifetime she was better known for her essays and historical novels. After reading Tolstoy she felt an urge to help the poor, and began to teach in her home. She started a class in English Literature at a Working Women's College, and was so popular there that after her death the pupils refused to go on with another teacher.

'I Saw a Stable'

I saw a stable, low and very bare,
　　A little child in a manger.
The oxen knew him, had him in their care,
　　To men he was a stranger.
The safety of the world was lying there,
　　And the world's danger.

There

There, in that other world, what waits for me?
What shall I find after that other birth?
No stormy, tossing, foaming, smiling sea,
　　But a new earth.

No sun to mark the changing of the days,
No slow, soft falling of the alternate night,
No moon, no star, no light upon my ways,
　　Only the Light.

No grey cathedral, wide and wondrous fair,
That I may tread where all my fathers trod.
Nay, nay, my soul, no house of God is there,
　　But only God.

RUDYARD KIPLING

1865–1936

Often labelled 'the typical Englishman', Kipling was actually born in India, where his father taught at the Bombay School of Art. After going to school in England he returned to India as a journalist. There he published seventy short stories in three years, and went on to write dialect poems for adults, and children's books such as 'The Jungle Book'. His many and varied writings earned him the Nobel Prize for Literature in 1907, and numerous other awards, including eight honorary degrees. Kipling's journalism took him to America, where he married, and to South Africa. But England remained his first love. His fervent patriotism was ridiculed in a cartoon showing Britannia as his girlfriend; but it was also the foundation of his enormous popularity.

The Glory of the Garden

Then seek your job with thankfulness and work till further orders,
If it's only netting strawberries or killing slugs on borders;
And when your back stops aching and your hands begin to harden,
You will find yourself a partner in the Glory of the Garden.

Oh, Adam was a gardener, and God who made him sees
That half a proper gardener's work is done upon his knees,
So when your work is finished, you can wash your hands and
    pray
For the Glory of the Garden, that it may not pass away!
And the Glory of the Garden it shall never pass away!

Non Nobis Domine

Non nobis Domine! –
   Not unto us, O Lord!
The Praise or Glory be
   Of any deed or word;
For in thy Judgment lies
   To crown or bring to nought
All knowledge or device
   That Man has reached or wrought.

And we confess our blame –
   How all too high we hold
That noise which men call Fame,
   That dross which men call Gold.
For these we undergo
   Our hot and godless days,
But in our hearts we know
   Not unto us the Praise.

O Power by whom we live –
   Creator, Judge, and Friend,
Upholdingly forgive
   Nor fail us at the end:
But grant us well to see
   In all our piteous ways –
Non nobis Domine! –
   Not unto us the Praise!

G.K. CHESTERTON

1874–1936

Gilbert Keith Chesterton started his first journalistic venture, a magazine called 'The Debater', as a pupil at St Paul's School, London. By the end of his life he had written 100 volumes of the most varied kind: collections of his weekly magazine essays, books of verse, religious and social comment, a history of England, and crime stories involving the eccentric detective-priest, Father Brown. Chesterton was a huge, unkempt, flamboyant character with a great sense of fun who was often caricatured. But he was also very popular, especially as an after-dinner speaker. He was received into the Roman Catholic church in 1922 greatly to the surprise of many who had thought he was a Catholic all the time!

The Happy Man

To teach the grey earth like a child,
   To bid the heavens repent,
I only ask from Fate the gift
   Of one man well content.

Him will I find: though when in vain
   I search the feast and mart,
The fading flowers of liberty,
   The painted masks of art.

I only find him at the last,
   On one old hill where nod
Golgotha's ghastly trinity –
   Three persons and one god.

The Donkey

When fishes flew and forests walked
　And figs grew upon thorn,
Some moment when the moon was blood
　Then surely I was born.

With monstrous head and sickening cry
　And ears like errant wings,
The devil's walking parody
　On all four-footed things.

The tattered outlaw of the earth,
　Of ancient crooked will;
Starve, scourge, deride me: I am dumb,
　I keep my secret still.

Fools! For I also had my hour;
　One far fierce hour and sweet:
There was a shout about my ears,
　And palms before my feet.

G.A. STUDDERT KENNEDY

1883–1929

Innumerable anecdotes have been told about Geoffrey Antekell Studdert Kennedy, the First World War chaplain from Leeds whose habit of giving away Woodbine cigarettes to the soldiers earned him the nickname 'Woodbine Willie'. He was incredibly absent-minded, leaving a trail of toothbrushes and pyjamas behind him! And he was extraordinarily generous – even to giving away his overcoat. He spoke with an Irish accent, gained at school in Dublin, and swore freely – sometimes in his sermons! He was much-loved, especially for his down-to-earth approach to faith. 'There comes a time in every man's life,' he said in one sermon, 'when he must wonder what the hell it is all about.'

Kennedy's 'Rough Rhymes of a Padre', mostly written in dialect, are a vivid record of what war means to the common soldier.

Waste

Waste of Muscle, waste of Brain,
Waste of Patience, waste of Pain,
Waste of Manhood, waste of Health,
Waste of Beauty, waste of Wealth,
Waste of Blood, and waste of Tears,
Waste of Youth's most precious years,
Waste of ways the Saints have trod,
Waste of Glory, waste of God, –
       War!

'My Peace I Give Unto You'

Blessed are the eyes that see
   The things that you have seen,
Blessed are the feet that walk
   The ways where you have been.

Blessed are the eyes that see
   The Agony of God,
Blessed are the feet that tread
   The paths his feet have trod.

Blessed are the souls that solve
   The paradox of Pain,
And find the path that, piercing it,
   Leads through to Peace again.

Work

Close by the careless worker's side,
   Still patient stands
The Carpenter of Nazareth,
   With pierced hands
Outstretched to plead unceasingly,
   His love's demands.

Longing to pick the hammer up
   And strike a blow,
Longing to feel his plane swing out,
   Steady and slow,
The fragrant shavings falling down,
   Silent as snow.

Because this is my work, O Lord,
   It must be thine,
Because it is a human task
   It is divine.
Take me, and brand me with thy cross,
   Thy slave's proud sign.

Indifference

When Jesus came to Golgotha they hanged him on a tree,
They drave great nails through hands and feet, and made a Calvary;
They crowned him with a crown of thorns, red were his wounds and deep,
For those were crude and cruel days, the human flesh was cheap.

When Jesus came to Birmingham, they simply passed him by,
They never hurt a hair of him, they only let him die;
For men had grown more tender, and they would not give him pain,
They only passed down the street, and left him in the rain.

Still Jesus cried, 'Forgive them, for they know not what they do,'
And still it rained the winter rain that drenched him through and through;
The crowds went home and left the streets without a soul to see,
And Jesus crouched against a wall and cried for Calvary.

'When Through the Whirl of Wheels'

When through the whirl of wheels, and engines humming,
Patiently powerful for the sons of men,
Peals like a trumpet promise of his coming,
Who in the clouds is pledged to come again;

When through the night the furnace fires a-flaring,
Shooting out tongues of flame like leaping blood,
Speak to the heart of Love, alive and daring,
Sing of the boundless energy of God;

When in the depths the patient miner striving,
Feels in his arms the vigour of the Lord,
Strikes for a kingdom and his King's arriving,
Holding his pick more splendid than the sword;

When on the sweat of labour and its sorrow,
Toiling in twilight flickering and dim,
Flames out the sunshine of the great tomorrow,
When all the world looks up because of him –

Then will he come with meekness for his glory,
God in a workman's jacket as before,
Living again th'eternal gospel story,
Sweeping the shavings from his work-shop floor.

The Rose

There is a world of wonder in this rose;
God made it, and his whole creation grows
To a point of perfect beauty
In this garden plot. He knows
The poet's thrill
On this June morning, as he sees
His will
To beauty taking form, his word
Made flesh, and dwelling among men.
All mysteries
In this one flower meet
And intertwine,
The universal is concrete
The human and divine,
In one unique and perfect thing, are fused
Into a unity of Love,
This rose as I behold it;
For all things gave it me,
The stars have helped to mould it,
The air, soft moonshine, and the rain,
The meekness of old mother earth,
The many-billowed sea.
The evolution of ten million years,
And all the pain
Of ages, brought it to its birth
And gave it me.
The tears
Of Christ are in it
And his blood
Has dyed it red,
I could not see it but for him
Because he led
Me to the love of God,
From which all beauty springs.
I and my rose
Are one.

DAME EDITH SITWELL
1887–1964

The author of a book on 'The English Eccentrics', Dame Edith – an imposing six feet tall, and impressive with it – was herself a great eccentric. Joyce Grenfell tells of an early television interview, soon after Dame Edith had become a Christian:

'She looked splendid. Her gothic appearance, her long and beautiful hands covered with many giant aquamarine rings, made a fascinating picture.' When asked why she had come to faith, 'she said she had looked at the pattern of a frost flower on a window-pane; she had studied shells, feathers, petals and grasses; and she knew, without a doubt, that there must be a cause ... "I have come to believe that the cause is God".'

Dame Edith grew up on the family estate in Yorkshire. Her brothers Osbert and Sacheverell also became poets. From 1916–21 she edited 'Wheels', an anthology of modern verse. She then published several collections of her own decidedly individual and often incomprehensible poetry. When her recitation 'Facade', with music by William Walton, was first performed in London it caused a near-riot.

Still Falls the Rain
The Raids, 1940. Night and Dawn

Still falls the Rain –
Dark as the world of man, black as our loss –
Blind as the nineteen hundred and forty nails
Upon the Cross.

Still falls the Rain
With a sound like the pulse of the heart that is changed to the
   hammer-beat
In the Potter's Field, and the sound of the impious feet

On the Tomb:
        Still falls the Rain
In the Field of Blood where the small hopes breed and the human
   brain
Nurtures its greed, that worm with the brow of Cain.

Still falls the Rain
At the feet of the Starved Man hung upon the Cross.
Christ that each day, each night, nails there, have mercy on us –
On Dives and on Lazarus:
Under the Rain the sore and the gold are as one.

Still falls the Rain –
Still falls the Blood from the Starved Man's wounded Side:
He bears in His Heart all wounds, – those of the light that died,
The last faint spark
In the self-murdered heart, the wounds of the sad uncomprehend-
    ing dark,
The wounds of the baited bear, –
The blind and weeping bear whom the keepers beat
On his helpless flesh . . . the tears of the hunted hare.

Still falls the Rain –
Then – O Ile leape up to my God: who pulles me doune –
See, see where Christ's blood streames in the firmament:

It flows from the Brow we nailed upon the tree
Deep to the dying, to the thirsting heart
That holds the fires of the world, – dark-smirched with pain
As Caesar's laurel crown.

Then sounds the voice of One who like the heart of man
Was once a child who among beasts has lain –
'Still do I love, still shed my innocent light, my Blood, for thee.'

EDWIN MUIR
1887–1959

Edwin Muir was born on a farm in the Orkney Islands, off the north coast of Scotland. When he was fourteen the family moved to a poor area of Glasgow, where two of his brothers died. Muir became a clerk in a beer-bottling factory and then in a bone-processing plant. His experiences there made him a Socialist, and he went to London to work on the political periodical 'The New Age'.

He was thirty-five before he began to write poetry. Muir had a Christian upbringing, but it was late in life, following a mystical experience of Christ, that he made his faith truly his own. His poems translate that experience into his own imaginative language of myth and symbol.

Abraham

The rivulet-loving wanderer Abraham
Through waterless wastes tracing his fields of pasture
Led his Chaldean herds and fattening flocks
With the meandering art of wavering water
That seeks and finds, yet does not know its way.
He came, rested and prospered, and went on,
Scattering behind him little pastoral kingdoms,
And over each one its own particular sky,
Not the great rounded sky through which he journeyed,
That went with him but when he rested changed.
His mind was full of names
Learned from strange peoples speaking alien tongues,
And all that was theirs one day he would inherit.
He died content and full of years, though still
The Promise had not come, and left his bones,
Far from his father's house, in alien Canaan.

The Animals

They do not live in the world,
Are not in time and space.
From birth to death hurled
No word do they have, not one
To plant a foot upon,
Were never in any place.

For with names the world was called
Out of the empty air,
With names was built and walled,
Line and circle and square,
Dust and emerald;
Snatched from deceiving death
By the articulate breath.

But these have never trod
Twice the familiar track,
Never never turned back
Into the memoried day.
All is new and near
In the unchanging Here
Of the fifth great day of God,
That shall remain the same,
Never shall pass away.

On the sixth day we came.

Frederick William Harvey was born in Gloucestershire. He served in the First World War, and while in a German prisoner-of-war camp he wrote the poem 'The Bugler', which became very popular for a short time. That poem, together with his two collections of verse published in 1917 and 1921, is now almost forgotten. But 'Ducks', has become a standard entry in children's anthologies. Its off-beat look at a neglected aspect of creation – God's humour – appeals just as much to adults.

From 'Ducks'

When God had finished the stars and whirl of coloured suns
He turned his mind from big things to fashion little ones,
Beautiful tiny things (like daisies) he made, and then
He made the comical ones in case the minds of men
   Should stiffen and become
   Dull, humourless and glum:
And so forgetful of their Maker be
As to take even themselves – *quite seriously.*
Caterpillars and cats are lively and excellent puns:
All God's jokes are good – even the practical ones!
And as for the duck, I think God must have smiled a bit
Seeing those bright eyes blink on the day he fashioned it.
And he's probably laughing still at the sound that came out of its bill!

T.S. ELIOT

1888–1965

Thomas Stearns Eliot is undoubtedly the greatest poet of the modern age. Yet, when his influential but very difficult poem 'The Waste Land' appeared in 1922, one critic called it 'the greatest hoax in English literature'. Eliot grew up in Missouri, and was educated at Harvard. Despite this, a friend described him as 'English in everything but accent and citizenship'. (Both of these he later acquired when he emigrated to London in 1915.) 'The Waste Land' had expressed his loss of faith in European civilization after the First World War. By 1928, however, he had found a real Christian faith. His later poems, particularly the 'Four Quartets' and his verse play, 'Murder in the Cathedral', show a deep Christian hope, as do his prose writings such as 'The Idea of a Christian Society'. In 1948 Eliot was awarded the Nobel Prize for Literature.

'What Life Have You'

(from 'The Rock')

What life have you if you have not life together?
There is no life that is not in community,
And no community not lived in praise of GOD.
Even the anchorite who meditates alone,
For whom the days and nights repeat the praise of GOD,
Prays for the Church, the Body of Christ incarnate.
And now you live dispersed on ribbon roads,
And no man knows or cares who is his neighbour
Unless his neighbour makes too much disturbance,
But all dash to and fro in motor cars,
Familiar with the roads and settled nowhere.
Nor does the family even move about together,
But every son would have his motor cycle,
And daughters ride away on casual pillions.

Much to cast down, much to build, much to restore;
Let the work not delay, time and the arm not waste;
Let the clay be dug from the pit, let the saw cut the stone,
Let the fire not be quenched in the forge.

Journey of the Magi

'A cold coming we had of it,
Just the worst time of the year
For a journey, and such a long journey:
The ways deep and the weather sharp,
The very dead of winter.'
And the camels galled, sore-footed, refractory,
Lying down in the melting snow.
There were times we regretted
The summer palaces on slopes, the terraces,
And the silken girls bringing sherbet.
Then the camel men cursing and grumbling
And running away, and wanting their liquor and women,
And the night-fires going out, and the lack of shelters,
And the cities hostile and the towns unfriendly
And the villages dirty and charging high prices:
A hard time we had of it.
At the end we preferred to travel all night,
Sleeping in snatches,
With the voices singing in our ears, saying
That this was all folly.

Then at dawn we came down to a temperate valley,
Wet, below the snow line, smelling of vegetation;
With a running stream and a water-mill beating the darkness,
And three trees on the low sky,
And an old white horse galloped away in the meadow.
Then we came to a tavern with vine-leaves over the lintel,
Six hands at an open door dicing for pieces of silver,
And feet kicking the empty wine-skins.
But there was no information, and so we continued
And arriving at evening, not a moment too soon
Finding the place; it was (you may say) satisfactory.

All this was a long time ago, I remember,
And I would do it again, but set down
This set down
This: were we led all that way for
Birth or Death? There was a Birth, certainly,
We had evidence and no doubt. I had seen birth and death,
But had thought they were different; this Birth was
Hard and bitter agony for us, like Death, our death.
We returned to our places, these Kingdoms,
But no longer at ease here, in the old dispensation,
With an alien people clutching their gods.
I should be glad of another death.

A Song For Simeon

Lord, the Roman hyacinths are blooming in bowls and
The winter sun creeps by the snow hills;
The stubborn reason has made stand.
My life is light, waiting for the death wind,
Like a feather on the back of my hand.
Dust in sunlight and memory in corners
Wait for the wind that chills towards the dead land.

Grant us thy peace.
I have walked many years in this city,
Kept faith and fast, provided for the poor,
Have given and taken honour and ease.
There went never any rejected from my door.
Who shall remember my house, where shall I live my children's children
When the time of sorrow is come?
They will take to the goat's path, and the fox's home,
Fleeing from the foreign faces and the foreign swords.

Before the time of cords and scourges and lamentation
Grant us thy peace.
Before the stations of the mountain of desolation,
Before the certain hour of maternal sorrow,
Now at this birth season of decease,
Let the Infant, the still unspeaking and unspoken Word,
Grant Israel's consolation
To one who has eighty years and no tomorrow.

According to thy word.
They shall praise Thee and suffer in every generation
With glory and derision,
Light upon light, mounting the saints' stair.
Not for me the martyrdom, the ecstasy of thought and prayer,
Not for me the ultimate vision.
Grant me thy peace
(And a sword shall pierce thy heart,
Thine also).
I am tired with my own life and the lives of those after me,
I am dying in my own death and the deaths of those after me.
Let thy servant depart,
Having seen thy salvation.

C.S. LEWIS
1898–1963

After a childhood in Northern Ireland, Clive Staples Lewis studied at Oxford University where he became a Fellow of Magdalen College, and later Professor of Medieval and Renaissance English at Cambridge. His path to Christianity was long and slow, and he called himself 'perhaps the most dejected and reluctant convert in all England'. Nevertheless he went on to write several brilliant and very readable books arguing in defence of his faith. He is best known, however, for his 'Screwtape Letters', the correspondence of a senior devil to a junior one; and the 'Narnia Chronicles', seven children's books about a fictional country in which Christ is symbolized by the lion Aslan. Late in life Lewis married an American who was dying of cancer, and their brief but happy marriage called forth some of his most penetrating writing on suffering.

The Late Passenger

The sky was low, the sounding rain was falling dense and dark,
And Noah's sons were standing at the window of the Ark.

The beasts were in, but Japhet said, 'I see one creature more
Belated and unmated there come knocking at the door.'

'Well let him knock,' said Ham, 'Or let him drown or learn to swim.
We're overcrowded as it is; we've got no room for him.'

'And yet it knocks, how terribly it knocks,' said Shem, 'Its feet
Are hard as horn – but oh the air that comes from it is sweet.'

'Now hush,' said Ham, 'You'll waken Dad, and once he comes to see
What's at the door, it's sure to mean more work for you and me.'

Noah's voice came roaring from the darkness down below,
'Some animal is knocking. Take it in before we go.'

Ham shouted back, and savagely he nudged the other two,
'That's only Japhet knocking down a brad-nail in his shoe.'

Said Noah, 'Boys, I hear a noise that's like a horse's hoof.'
Said Ham, 'Why, that's the dreadful rain that drums upon the roof.'

Noah tumbled up on deck and out he put his head;
His face went grey, his knees were loosed, he tore his beard and said,

'Look, look! It would not wait. It turns away. It takes its flight.
Fine work you've made of it, my sons, between you all to-night!

'Even if I could outrun it now, it would not turn again
— Not now. Our great discourtesy has earned its high disdain.

'Oh noble and unmated beast, my sons were all unkind;
In such a night what stable and what manger will you find?

'Oh golden hoofs, oh cataracts of man, oh nostrils wide
With indignation! Oh the neck wave-arched, the lovely pride!

'Oh long shall be the furrows ploughed across the hearts of men
Before it comes to stable and to manger once again,

'And dark and crooked all the ways in which our race shall walk,
And shrivelled all their manhood like a flower with broken stalk,

'And all the world, oh Ham, may curse the hour when you were born;
Because of you the Ark must sail without the Unicorn.'

The Nativity

Among the oxen (like an ox I'm slow)
I see a glory in the stable grow
Which, with the ox's dullness might at length
      Give me an ox's strength.

Among the asses (stubborn I as they)
I see my Saviour where I looked for hay;
So may my beastlike folly learn at least
      The patience of a beast.

Among the sheep (I like a sheep have strayed)
I watch the manger where my Lord is laid;
Oh that my baa-ing nature would win thence
      Some woolly innocence!

Eden's Courtesy

Such natural love twixt beast and man we find
That children all desire an animal book,
And all brutes, not perverted from their kind,
Woo us with whinny, tongue, tail, song, or look;
   So much of Eden's courtesy yet remains.
But when a creature's dread, or mine, has built
A wall between, I think I feel the pains
That Adam earned and do confess my guilt.
   For till I tame sly fox and timorous hare
And lording lion in my self, no peace
Can be without; but after, I shall dare
Uncage the shadowy zoo and war will cease;
   Because the brutes within, I do not doubt,
Are archetypal of the brutes without.

SIR JOHN BETJEMAN

born 1906

John Betjeman has succeeded in being that rare thing, a truly popular poet who is more than a writer of light verse. In recognition of his success he was knighted in 1969 and he has been the English Poet Laureate since 1972. Of Dutch descent, he chose not to go into the family firm which designed furniture, glassware and silver. Instead his background in the visual arts gave him a boundless enthusiasm for architecture. His passionate campaigning to preserve England's Victorian heritage has earned him the nickname 'the bard of the railway gas-lamp'. He edited the 'Architectural Review' for some years, after a period as an unsuccessful teacher — related in his verse autobigraphy, 'Summoned by Bells'. Betjeman loves the ritual of the English church as much as its buildings.

Christmas

The bells of waiting Advent ring,
   The Tortoise stove is lit again
And lamp-oil light across the night
   Has caught the streaks of winter rain
In many a stained-glass window sheen
From Crimson Lake to Hooker's Green.

The holly in the windy hedge
   And round the Manor House the yew
Will soon be stripped to deck the ledge,
   The altar, font and arch and pew,
So that the villagers can say
'The church looks nice' on Christmas Day.

Provincial public houses blaze
   And Corporation tramcars clang,
On lighted tenements I gaze
   Where paper decorations hang,
And bunting in the red Town Hall
Says 'Merry Christmas to you all.'

And London shops on Christmas Eve
    Are strung with silver bells and flowers
As hurrying clerks the City leave
    To pigeon-haunted classic towers,
And marbled clouds go scudding by
The many-steepled London sky.

And girls in slacks remember Dad,
    And oafish louts remember Mum,
And sleepless children's hearts are glad,
    And Christmas-morning bells say 'Come!'
Even to shining ones who dwell
Safe in the Dorchester Hotel.

And is it true? And is it true,
    This most tremendous tale of all,
Seen in a stained-glass window's hue,
    A Baby in an ox's stall?
The Maker of the stars and sea
Become a Child on earth for me?

And is it true? For if it is,
    No loving fingers tying strings
Around those tissued fripperies,
    The sweet and silly Christmas things,
Bath salts and inexpensive scent
And hideous tie so kindly meant,

No love that in a family dwells,
    No carolling in frosty air,
Nor all the steeple-shaking bells
    Can with this single Truth compare –
That God was Man in Palestine
And lives today in Bread and Wine.

Before the Anaesthetic

or A Real Fright

Intolerably sad, profound
St Giles's bells are ringing round,
They bring the slanting summer rain
To tap the chestnut boughs again
Whose shadowy cave of rainy leaves
The gusty belfry-song receives.
Intolerably sad and true,
Victorian red and jewel blue,
The mellow bells are ringing round
And charge the evening light with sound,
And I look motionless from bed
On heavy trees and purple red
And hear the midland bricks and tiles
Throw back the bells of stone St Giles,
Bells, ancient now as castle walls,
Now hard and new as pitchpine stalls,
Now full with help from ages past,
Now dull with death and hell at last.
Swing up! and give me hope of life,
Swing down! and plunge the surgeon's knife.
I, breathing for a moment, see
Death wing himself away from me
And think, as on this bed I lie,
Is it extinction when I die?
I move my limbs and use my sight;
Not yet, thank God, not yet the Night.
Oh better far those echoing hells
Half-threaten'd in the pealing bells
Than that this 'I' should cease to be –
Come quickly, Lord, come quick to me.
St Giles's bells are asking now
'And hast thou known the Lord, hast thou?'
St Giles's bells, they richly ring
'And was that Lord our Christ the King?'
St Giles's bells they hear me call
I never knew the Lord at all.
Oh not in me your Saviour dwells
You ancient, rich St Giles's bells.
Illuminated missals – spires –
Wide screens and decorated quires –
All these I loved, and on my knees
I thanked myself for knowing these
And watched the morning sunlight pass
Through richly stained Victorian glass

And in the colour-shafted air
I, kneeling, thought the Lord was there.
Now, lying in the gathering mist
I know that Lord did not exist;
Now, lest this 'I' should cease to be,
Come, real Lord, come quick to me.
With every gust the chestnut sighs,
With every breath a mortal dies;
The man who smiled alone, alone,
And went his journey on his own
With 'Will you give my wife this letter,
In case, of course, I don't get better?'
Waits for his coffin lid to close
On waxen head and yellow toes,
Almighty Saviour, had I Faith
There'd be no fight with kindly Death.
Intolerably long and deep
St Giles's bells swing on in sleep:
'But still you go from here alone'
Say all the bells about the Throne.

W.H. AUDEN

1907–1973

Born in England and educated at Oxford, Wystan Hugh Auden was a leading poet of his generation. His first book of poems was published in 1930. In 1939 he emigrated to the United States, and later became an American citizen. From 1956–1961 he was Professor of Poetry at Oxford University. His early work sounds a note of protest and social criticism. 'About the House' (1966) reflects a definite Christian commitment.

At the Manger Mary Sings

O shut your bright eyes that mine must endanger
With their watchfulness; protected by its shade
Escape from my care: what can you discover
From my tender look but how to be afraid?
Love can but confirm the more it would deny.
   Close your bright eye.

Sleep. What have you learned from the womb that bore you
But an anxiety your Father cannot feel?
Sleep. What will the flesh that I gave do for you,
Or my mother love, but tempt you from his will?
Why was I chosen to teach his Son to weep?
   Little One, sleep.

Dream. In human dreams earth ascends to heaven
Where no one need pray nor ever feel alone.
In your first few hours of life here, O have you
Chosen already what death must be your own?
How soon will you start on the Sorrowful Way?
   Dream while you may.

NORMAN NICHOLSON

born 1914

Norman Nicholson still lives in the house where he was born, in the small industrial town of Millom in the English Lake District. His home is only fifteen miles from the Lakeland of Wordsworth, Coleridge and Southey. He is very much a poet of that area, drawing his imagery from the local environment. He sees the small isolated town as a microcosm of society. Norman Nicholson is the author of a number of books of poetry, novels and plays, and has edited an anthology of religious verse. 'Unfashionably direct' in language and in the expression of his Christian faith, he is recognized as one of the finest landscape poets of our day.

The Burning Bush

When Moses, musing in the desert, found
The thorn bush spiking up from the hot ground,
And saw the branches, on a sudden, bear
The crackling yellow barberries of fire,

He searched his learning and imagination
For any logical, neat explanation,
And turned to go, but turned again and stayed,
And faced the fire and knew it for his God.

I too have seen the briar alight like coal,
The love that burns, the flesh that's ever whole,
And many times have turned and left it there,
Saying: 'It's prophecy – but metaphor'.

But stinging tongues like John the Baptist shout:
'That this is metaphor is no way out.
It's dogma too, or you make God a liar;
The bush is still a bush, and fire is fire'.

SYDNEY CARTER

born 1915

Folk-singer, performing poet, hymnwriter, satirist — Sydney Carter refuses to fit neatly into one category. He emerged as a popular songwriter during the 1960s when folk became allied with protest. Some of his songs are political satires, such as 'I want to have a little bomb like you'. Some express Christianity in a new way or, like 'When I needed a neighbour', draw on the tradition of the Negro spiritual. Some, like 'Down Below', which celebrates London's sewerage system, are just plain fun. They are, as he points out, 'not always welcomed in a church ... most come off better in the cellar or crypt'. As well as writing songs he has been a teacher and served in the Friends' Ambulance Unit in the Middle East and Greece. He now lives in south London.

The Faith Came First

The faith came first.
In the beginning was
the way that I believe
and after that
came all that I believe in

Hitler, Christ,
Apollo, Aphrodite
and Karl Marx
fruit, thorn or
flower on
a single tree.
Faith is the sap of it.

By faith I test
the gospel of St Matthew,
Michelangelo,
Bach or the Beatles
but
the faith came first, I see
no other rock
but this to
build upon.

JACK CLEMO

born 1916

Jack Clemo has never moved from the little cottage where he was born, among the Cornish clay-pits which have been the main inspiration for his poetry. As a young man he was by his own description a 'pagan mystic'. His conversion owes much to the simple faith of his mother Eveline, with whom he lived until her death in her eighties. Deaf for forty years and blind for twenty-five, Clemo was convinced that he would marry in spite of these handicaps. In 1968 his faith was answered when he married Ruth Peaty (his mother was still alive to see her son's wedding). The story of his search for this fulfilment is told in the second part of his autobiography, 'The Marriage of a Rebel', published in 1980.

The Winds

There is a tree grows upside down,
    Its roots are in the sky;
Its lower branches reach the earth
    When amorous winds are nigh.

On one lone bough there starkly hangs
    A Man just crucified,
And all the other branches bear
    The choice fruits of the Bride.

When Pleasure's wind goes frisking past,
    Unhallowed by a prayer,
It swirls dead leaves from earth-born trees,
    Old growths of pride and care.

The gracious fruits are hidden by
    These leaves of human stain;
The Crucified beneath his load
    Shudders, as if in pain.

But swift springs down a credal wind,
    It thrills through all the boughs;
The dead leaves scatter and are lost;
    The Christ renews his vows.

Christ in the Clay-pit

Why should I find him here
And not in a church, nor yet
Where Nature heaves a breast like Olivet
Against the stars? I peer
Upon his footsteps in this quarried mud;
I see his blood
In rusty stains on pit-props, waggon-frames
Bristling with nails, not leaves. There were no leaves
Upon his chosen Tree,
No parasitic flowering over shames
Of Eden's primal infidelity.

Just splintered wood and nails
Were fairest blossoming for him who speaks
Where mica-silt outbreaks
Like water from the side of his own clay
In that strange day
When he was pierced. Here still the earth-face pales
And rends in earthquake roarings of a blast
With tainted rock outcast
While fields and woods lie dreaming yet of peace
'Twixt God and his creation, of release
From potent wrath – a faith that waxes bold
In churches nestling snugly in the fold
Of scented hillsides where mild shadows brood.
The dark and stubborn mood
Of him whose feet are bare upon this mire,
And in the furnace fire
Which hardens all the clay that has escaped,
Would not be understood
By worshippers of beauty toned and shaped
To flower or hymn. I know their facile praise
False to the heart of me, which like this pit
Must still be disembowelled of Nature's stain,
And rendered fit
By violent mouldings through the tunnelled ways
Of all he would regain.

MADELEINE L'ENGLE

born 1919

After Madeleine L'Engle had written five adult novels, her inspiration suddenly dried up. She published nothing for ten years. To support their family her actor husband left the stage and together they ran the local general stores. When she began to write again, this time for children, she had nothing but rejection slips. But when her fantasy 'A Wrinkle in Time' finally found a publisher, it immediately won the Newbery Award, America's highest honour for children's fiction. Since then several other successful children's books have followed. Miss L'Engle works as librarian and writer-in-residence at the Cathedral of St John the Divine, New York. At one time an atheist, she now finds her Christian faith is deepened by new discoveries in science, which also inspire her writing.

O Simplicitas

An angel came to me
And I was unprepared
To be what God was using.
Mother I was to be.
A moment I despaired,
Thought briefly of refusing.
The angel knew I heard.
According to God's Word
I bowed to this strange choosing.

A palace should have been
The birthplace of a king
(I had no way of knowing).
We went to Bethlehem;
It was so strange a thing.
The wind was cold, and blowing,
My cloak was old, and thin.
They turned us from the inn;
The town was overflowing.

God's Word, a child so small,
Who still must learn to speak,
Lay in humiliation.
Joseph stood, strong and tall.
The beasts were warm and meek
And moved with hesitation.
The Child born in a stall?
I understood it: all.
Kings came in adoration.

Perhaps it was absurd:
The stable set apart,
The sleepy cattle lowing;
And the incarnate Word
Resting against my heart.
My joy was overflowing.
The shepherds came, adored
The folly of the Lord,
Wiser than all men's knowing.

JOHN BENNETT
born 1920

John Bennett is Professor of English at St Norbert College, De Pere, Wisconsin. He has written a number of books of poetry and his poems have been published in 'The New Yorker', 'The New York Times' and other distinguished journals. 'In a time when rising poets have discovered the art of public relations ... he has gone his quiet way ... He has spent more time writing his poetry than promoting it.'

Pentecost

So free, so bright, so beautiful and fair,
the Holy Dove descends the earthly air:
in startling joyance come
from its immortal home,
it bears the Glory that all men may share.

Through ancient space and newest time, it brings
transcendent reason to a world of things:
It shows each mind and heart
how to assume its part
in dances born of God's imaginings.

On wings of subtlest flame, the Holy Dove
flies through the human world and offers love:
it teaches Heart and Mind
how to transcend their kind
and praise the God who lets all being move.

So free, so bright, so beautiful and fair,
the Holy Dove flies through the mortal air:
always there descending,
always there ascending,
it brings the Glory that all men may share.

EVANGELINE PATERSON

born 1928

One of the many new writers to emerge from the recent British revival of Christian interest in the arts, Evangeline Paterson has been writing poetry for a number of years. She grew up in Dublin but married an Englishman. With their three children they lived for eighteen years in St Andrew's, Scotland. She now lives in Leicester and is the organizer of a local group for Christian artists. She is co-editor of the magazine 'Other Poetry', and in 1980 won one of three major poetry prizes at the Cheltenham Literary Festival. She lists her hobbies as reading, writing and talking to people, but has also been known to relax with embroidery.

'And That Will Be Heaven'

and that will be heaven

and that will be heaven
at last   the first unclouded
seeing

    to stand like the sunflower
turned full face to the sun   drenched
in light   in the still centre
held   while the circling planets
hum with an utter joy
        seeing and knowing
at last   in every particle
seen and known   and not turning
away
    never turning away
again

Death on a Crossing

What he never thought to consider was whether
the thing was true. What bewildered him, mostly,
was the way that the rumours had of reaching him
from such improbable sources – illiterate pamphlets
pressed in his hand, the brash or the floundering stranger
who came to his door, the proclamations, among
so many others, on hoardings

                     though sometimes waking
a brief dismay, that never quite prodded him
to the analyst's couch.

               But annunciations, he thought,
should come to a rational man in a rational way.
He walked between a skyful of midnight angels
and a patch on somebody's jeans, both saying
the same thing to his stopped ears

                  till the day
when he stepped on a crossing with not enough conviction
to get him safe to the other side, and he lay
among strangers' feet, and the angels lowered their trumpets
and no sweet chariot swung, to carry him home.

LUCI SHAW

born 1928

Luci Shaw spent her childhood in England, Australia and Canada. She took a degree at Wheaton College in the United States and is married to an American. Together they run their own publishing house. They live 'on an acre of oaks and black walnuts' in West Chicago, Illinois. Luci Shaw's work has appeared widely in journals and magazines. Her first book of poems, 'Listen to the Green', was published in 1971, 'The Secret Trees' in 1976 and 'The Sighting' in 1981.

Small Song

God of the sky,
God of the sea,
God of the rock
and bird and tree,
you are also
the God of me.

The pebble fell.
The water stirred
and stilled again.
The hidden bird
made song for you.
His praise you heard.

You heard him sing
from in the tree.
And searching still
I know you'll see
the love that wings
to you from me.

May 20: Very Early Morning

all the field praises him/all
dandelions are his glory/gold
and silver all trilliums unfold
white flames above their trinities
of leaves all wild strawberries
and massed wood violets reflect his skies—
clean blue and white
all brambles/all oxeyes
all stalks and stems lift to his light
all young windflower bells
tremble on hair
springs for his air's
carillon touch/last year's yarrow (raising
brittle star skeletons) tells
age is not past praising
all small low unknown
unnamed weeds show his impossible greens
all grasses sing
tone on clear tone
all mosses spread a spring-
soft velvet for his feet
and by all means
all leaves/buds/all flowers cup
jewels of fire and ice
holding up
to his kind morning heat
a silver sacrifice

now
make of our hearts a field
to raise your praise

JOHN UPDIKE

born 1932

'I began as a writer of light verse,' Updike says. He is in fact better known for his novels and short stories. Born at Shillington, Pennsylvania, he worked for a short time as a staff reporter for 'The New Yorker'. He has a family of four children, and now lives at Ipswich, Massachusetts.

Seven Stanzas at Easter

Make no mistake if he rose at all
it was as his body;
if the cells' dissolution did not reverse, the molecules reknit,
    the amino acids rekindle,
the church will fall.

It was not as the flowers,
each soft Spring recurrent;
it was not as his Spirit in the mouths and fuddled eyes of the
    eleven apostles;
it was as his flesh: ours.

The same hinged thumbs and toes,
the same valved heart
that – pierced – died, withered, decayed, and then regathered
    out of his Father's might
new strength to enclose.

Let us not mock God with metaphor,
analogy, sidestepping transcendence;
making of the event a parable, a sign painted in the faded
    credulity of earlier ages:
let us walk through the door.

The stone is rolled back, not papier-mâché,
not a stone in a story,
but the vast rock of materiality that in the slow grinding
    of time will eclipse for each of us
the wide light of day.

And if we will have an angel at the tomb,
make it a real angel,
weighty with Max Planck's quanta, vivid with hair, opaque
      in the dawn light, robed in real linen
spun on a definite loom.

Let us not seek to make it less monstrous,
for our own convenience, our own sense of beauty,
lest, awakened in one unthinkable hour, we are embarrassed
      by the miracle,
and crushed by remonstrance.

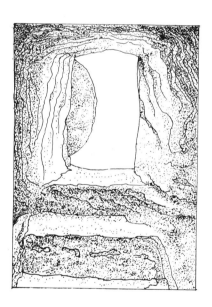

E.W. OLDENBURG

1936–1974

William Oldenburg was born in Muskegon, Michigan. He began writing poems in 1967, 'forced into it by agreeing to teach a creative writing course'. That compulsion soon became an addiction. He continued as a teacher and professor of English to publish poems in a number of magazines. His work has also been included in a number of anthologies. He was killed in a car accident in 1974.

In Canterbury Cathedral

On a day sweet with April showers
the safe tires of our tour bus
had sung us south from London,

Sightseer pilgrims, cameras slung,
no need or time on patient plodding
horses for long diverting tales.

We stood at last at Beckett's shrine,
lost in architecture and dates,
confused by Norman and Gothic.

Our ancient tiny guide seemed shrunk
into his suit, dwarfed by his clothes
as we all were dwarfed by time.

His small precise English voice went on:
pronounced 'Our Lord,' and the words
fell on us like a benediction.

'Our' – incredible assumption of union
offered in passing to American strangers,
mortar for diverse motley stones.

Time and blood and history redeemed
from meaninglessness: two words
turned sightseers into pilgrims.

STEVE TURNER

born 1949

Steve Turner has been writing poetry since 1965 and has given poetry readings in both Britain and America. 'At last,' wrote Peter Lewis in a British national daily newspaper, 'a poet who captures today with all the flair of a rock number.' The image is an appropriate one: Steve has in fact written numerous articles on rock music. His poetry has appeared in a number of well-known secular magazines — 'Over 21', 'She', 'Cosmopolitan'. The two poems below are from his latest book, 'Nice and Nasty'.

How to Hide Jesus

There are people after Jesus.
They have seen the signs.
Quick, let's hide him.
Let's think; carpenter,
         fishermen's friend,
         disturber of religious comfort.
Let's award him a degree in theology,
a purple cassock
and a position of respect.
They'll never think of looking here.
Let's think;
His dialect may betray him,
His tongue is of the masses.
Let's teach him Latin
and seventeenth century English,
they'll never think of listening in.
Let's think;
humble,
Man of Sorrows,
nowhere to lay his head.
We'll build a house for him,
somewhere away from the poor.
We'll fill it with brass and silence.
It's sure to throw them off.

There are people after Jesus.
Quick, let's hide him.

Christmas is Really For the Children

Christmas is really
for the children.
Especially for children
who like animals, stables,
stars and babies wrapped
in swaddling clothes.
Then there are wise men,
kings in fine robes,
humble shepherds and a
hint of rich perfume.

Easter is not really
for the children
unless accompanied by a
cream filled egg.
It has whips, blood, nails,
a spear and allegations
of body snatching.
It involves politics, God
and the sins of the world.
It is not good for people
of a nervous disposition.
They would do better to
think on rabbits, chickens
and the first snowdrop
of spring.
Or they'd do better to
wait for a re-run of
Christmas without asking
too many questions about
what Jesus did when he grew up
or whether there's any connection.

When through the whirl of wheels, and engines
   humming 87
When will you ever, Peace, wild wooddove, shy
   wings shut 72
Whither, midst falling dew 49

Who would true valour see 37
Wilt thou forgive that sin where I begun 20
Wilt thou not visit me? 54
Why should I find him here 111
Yet if his Majesty, our sovereign Lord 30

ACKNOWLEDGEMENTS

The following poems are copyright and are
included by kind permission of the copyright holders

Rudyard Kipling, 'The Glory of the Garden' and 'Non Nobis Domine' reprinted by permission of The National Trust and A.P. Watt. For USA: 'The Glory of the Garden', copyright 1911 by Rudyard Kipling and 'Non Nobis Domine' copyright 1934 by Rudyard Kipling; both poems from *Rudyard Kipling's Verse: Definitive Edition* reprinted by permission of The National Trust and Doubleday & Company, Inc.

G.K. Chesterton, 'The Donkey' and 'The Happy Man' reprinted by permission of the Estate of G.K. Chesterton and J.M. Dent and Sons Ltd. For USA: reprinted by permission of Dodd, Mead & Company, Inc. from *The Collected Poems of G.K. Chesterton*, copyright 1932 by Dodd, Mead and Company, Inc. (copyright renewed 1959 by Oliver Chesterton).

Edith Sitwell, 'Still Falls the Rain', reprinted by permission of David Higham Associates Ltd from *Collected Poems* published by Macmillan.

Edwin Muir, 'Abraham' and 'The Animals', reprinted by permission of Faber and Faber Ltd from *The Collected Poems of Edwin Muir*. For USA: reprinted by permission of Oxford University Press, Inc. from *Collected Poems* by Edwin Muir, copyright © 1960 Willa Muir.

F.W. Harvey, extract from 'Ducks' reprinted by permission of Sidgwick of Jackson Ltd.

T.S. Eliot, extract from 'The Rock', 'Journey of the Magi' and 'A Song for Simeon', reprinted by permission of

Faber and Faber Ltd from *Collected Poems 1909–1962* by T.S. Eliot. For USA: from *Collected Poems 1909–1962* by T.S. Eliot, copyright 1936 by Harcourt Brace Janovich, Inc.; copyright © 1963, 1964 by T.S. Eliot; reprinted by permission of the publisher.

C.S. Lewis, 'The Late Passenger', 'The Nativity' and 'Eden's Courtesy' reprinted by permission of Collins Publishers. For USA: reprinted by permission of Harcourt Brace Janovich, Inc. from *Poems* by C.S. Lewis, copyright © 1964 by the Executors of the Estate of C.S. Lewis

Sir John Betjeman, 'Christmas' and 'Before the Anaesthetic' reprinted by permission of John Murray (Publisher) Ltd and Houghton Miffin Co from *Collected Poems*.

W.H. Auden, 'At the Manger Mary Sings' reprinted by permission of Faber and Faber Ltd. For USA: reprinted by permission of Random House, Inc. from *W.H. Auden: Collected Poems*, edited by Edward Mendelson, copyright 1944, renewed 1972, by W.H. Auden.

Norman Nicholson, 'The Burning Bush', reprinted by permission of Faber and Faber Ltd from *Five Rivers* by Norman Nicholson.

Sydney Carter, 'The Faith Came First', reprinted by permission of Stainer and Bell Ltd from *The Two-way Clock*.

Jack Clemo, 'The Winds' and 'Christ in the Clay-pit' reprinted by permission of Associated Book Publishers Ltd from *The Map of Clay*

by Jack Clemo, published by Eyre Methuen.

Madeleine L'Engle, 'O Simplicitas', reprinted by permission of Harold Shaw Publishers from *Weather of the Heart*,copyright © 1978, Crosswicks.

John Bennett, 'Pentecost', reprinted by permission of William B. Eerdmans Publishing Co.

Evangeline Paterson, 'And That will be Heaven' and 'Death on a Crossing', reprinted by permission of the author.

Luci Shaw, 'Small Song' reprinted from *Listen to the Green* © Luci Shaw 1971, Harold Shaw Publishers; and 'May 20: Very Early Morning' reprinted from *The Secret Tree* © Luci Shaw 1976, Harold Shaw Publishers, by permission of the author.

John Updike, 'Seven Stanzas at Easter' reprinted by permission of Andre Deutsch Ltd from *Telephone Poles* by John Updike. For USA: reprinted by permission of Alfred Knopf, Inc. from *Telephone Poles and Other Poems* by John Updike.

E.W. Oldenburg, 'In Canterbury Cathedral' reprinted by permission of Harold Shaw Publishers from *Sightseers into Pilgrims*, edited Luci Shaw, copyright © 1973, Harold Shaw Publishers, USA.

Steve Turner, 'How to Hide Jesus' and 'Christmas is Really For The Children', reprinted by permission of Marshall, Morgan & Scott Publications Ltd, from *Nice and Nasty* by Steve Turner.